**By Barrett Tagli**

# Table of Contents



ISBN 978-0-634-08365-5

7777 W. Bluemound Rd. P.O. Box 13819 Milwaukee, WI 53213

In Australia Contact:
**Hal Leonard Australia Pty. Ltd.**
4 Lentara Court
Cheltenham, Victoria, 3192 Australia
Email: ausadmin@halleonard.com



Visit Hal Leonard Online at
**www.halleonard.com**

# Introduction

## What It Is

In any style, solos and melodies make use of the notes in the chords that are being played. In this book, well start from scratch and learn to find both the chord tones and the correct scales to go with them in any spot on the fretboard.

Part I is a very simple preview to show you where the book is going. Then all the scales, arpeggios, and theory you need are presented, explained, and drilled in Part II with exercises that have a rhythmic focus. This all serves to prepare you for the longer chord-tone soloing routines in Part III.

Pick up a guitar magazine or book and you'll find music being explained with a slew of numbers: "In measure 18, (insert amazing player here) sneaks in a stunning major 6th over the A♭, resolving to the 3rd of the I chord." Ever wonder if great players actually think of those numbers, or is it all just theoretical justification dreamed up afterwards? The answer is yes, they do think that way, even if they don't know all the terms used by the guy who writes about it later. Be it crude or sophisticated, much musicality comes from knowing how notes relate to the underlying chords. The numbers (and letters) are the language used to express this chord-related, or *harmonic*, information.

You might pick this up by trial and error, by relying on your ear, and/or by copying other players. This is necessary and desirable, and the way we all learn in the end, but you can cut down the time it takes to reach a professional level (where you're always ready to play something that fits the music) by applying harmonic theory to your practice. In other words, rather than reinvent the wheel, just steal it and run over those who came before you.

## Who It's For

This book is for players of any style, at all but the most beginning levels. I'll only assume you know the most basic techniques like strumming chords and picking single notes (techniques like bending strings, hammer-ons, and pull-offs are not needed for the program). Everything beyond that is explained in detail, from basic harmony and theory on up. But there's no mistaking that by the end of Part III the material is advanced, and you can expect to continue to use this book for years to come.

Once you have enough basics from Part II under your fingers, the routines in Part III will produce noticeable differences in your playing in just a few weeks. After a year of applying the method, you'll know how to solo melodically over anything but the most challenging chord progressions. With the concept in hand, you can then make sense of those magazine transcriptions, attack other books with intelligence, and use what you learn from them in your own music.

## Where It Came From

Students hear me soloing over tunes in different styles—rock, country, whatever. Sometimes they stop me and say, "Show me THAT lick!" I'd like to, but often I can't. There is not a giant mental library of licks that I simply plug in one after another. There are some licks to learn, of course, but there's more to it—some way of picking out notes on the fly so that they flow in a musical way, all in less time than it takes to think about it.

Then they might ask, "What scale did that come from?" or "Was that an arpeggio?" I explain that it's neither scale nor arpeggio, but sort of both at the same time, which leads us into a productive course of study, the refinement of which you now have before you.

We'll use lots of exercises for gradually learning to take the chords into consideration when soloing. These exercises are based on the most beneficial ones all my teachers showed me, with refinements added over the years. The purpose of each exercise may not always be immediately apparent, but I hope you will trust me and put in some time on them, as their goal is to train your reflexes to do things you may not have figured you'd need them to do.

### Where It's Going

The exercises in this book will help you acquire harmonic sense step by step, from the ground floor to the top of the skyscraper. Of course, having the chord-tone advantage will make you a better soloist, but there'll also be lots of useful side effects. It will help your rhythm playing. It'll make you a better composer. It will help your reading ability. It will make you sound more professional in any situation. You'll communicate with other musicians at an advanced level. Your musical knowledge will be deep, though not necessarily flashy (unless you want it to be).

All of this is a lot to ask from one little book, but the book has the easy job. You will have to practice consistently and with focus. It will be tough going at times, but if it were easy, everybody would be doing it already.

Speaking of "easy," congratulations are in order if you have the good fortune to be one for whom these things do come easily. I'm not one of those people. But neither luck nor talent are necessary to achieve the goals of this book. What I and every teacher wish for you are the greater blessings of desire and determination. No amount of luck or talent can overcome their lack.

# About the CD

For many of the exercises, tracks are included on the CD (labeled in the text with Track 10) so you can hear exactly how they should sound. When there is an example solo, it is panned to one side of the stereo field. Voiceovers of counting and chord-change announcements are also panned to one side. By turning your balance knob one way, you can remove the solo to play over the rhythm track yourself. By turning the knob the other way, you can practice playing chords behind the solo. Both skills are important. Although it's not the primary focus of this book, you should practice playing rhythm guitar just as much as soloing; it comprises most of the live and studio work of a professional guitarist. Record your own rhythm tracks (and your solos, if you can), and strive to make them as perfectly timed and cleanly executed as possible. Listening to these recordings can be painful at times, but it'll spur improvements in your playing.

**Tuning Pitches**

# Part I:

## A Preview to Soloing With Chord Tones

This is how I spend my first couple of private lessons with students who've already learned some licks note-for-note but now want to improvise more melodically on their own. There's a lot of playing and a little theory. We use chord tones over a simple two-chord jam, then over a basic three-chord blues.

By the time you've played through the step-by-step examples in these two chapters, you'll have a pretty good idea of how the rest of the book can help make you a monster player.

# 1 Let's Jam

I won't overwhelm you with music theory right off the bat. In fact, all of the theory in this book, while important, is secondary to practice. Sometimes playing helps the explanation make sense, so it's OK to try the exercises before fully understanding the theory. But you'll need to know why you're playing the notes as soon as you can, so you can apply the concepts to real songs.

## Targeting Roots

First play the chords below with a clean sound, strumming all six strings for the A chord and the top five strings for the D chord. Let your strums include the high notes, and try to make them ring out as clearly as possible. These are the notes we'll be emphasizing during the solo.

We'll hit a specific chord tone when each of the two chords is sounding. These are *target notes*. They're moving targets, because music is always moving, so you have to "pull the trigger" at the right time.

The root of each chord is our first target; it's the note that has the same name as the chord. I don't expect you to know all the names of the notes on the fretboard now, but the more you do these exercises, the better you'll be able to. Besides the obvious place on the bottom of the chord, there is an A on the fourth string, seventh fret. This note will be played over the A chord, using your third finger.

A root of the D chord is on the third string, also at the seventh fret, and also will be played with the third finger. Play the D note when the D chord is sounding.

Listen to the recorded solo over the chords, and then turn your balance knob to remove it from the mix and play exactly the same thing.

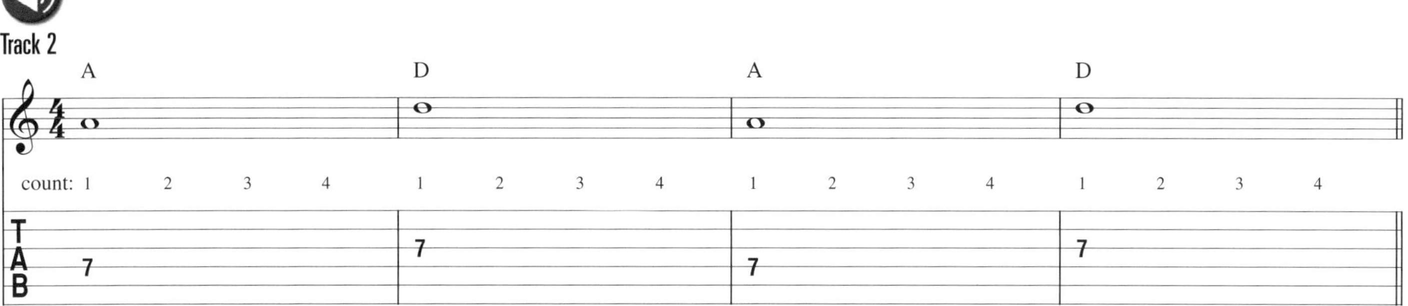


If you're really listening, you may notice there's a slight clash if you make a mistake and hit the D note over the A chord. It's not necessarily ugly, and in some situations such a clash is desirable, but for our purposes right now it is to be avoided. If you make the other obvious mistake and hit the A note over the D chord, you'll notice it sounds good. It just so happens that A is a chord tone of D, but D is not a chord tone of A. That's part of the beauty of music: some accidents sound nice. But not all of them do, so our goal is to gain control!

Instead of right and wrong, black and white, music spans a spectrum from consonant to dissonant, obvious to unexpected, which we control with our note choices. There are many gray areas where we'll have lots of freedom to decide what we want, and those decisions may change as our ears develop. Here at the beginning of the course, we're starting with the most obviously correct note choice: the root of each chord.

## Lead-Ins to Roots

Continue playing the notes A and D as before, and now lead in to each of them by playing a C on the fifth fret of string 3. (This lead-in note can be called a *pickup* note.) The lead-in should be played one beat in advance of the target notes. In other words, we continue to play the root of each chord on beat 1 along with the changing chord, and play a short C note immediately before it on beat 4. (We'll talk more about counting beats in Chapter 4.) Listen closely to the example, then dial out the lead guitar on the CD and play the same thing over the chords.

The C note leads smoothly down to A and up to D. Now let's expand our options for the lead-in notes. Let's also add G on the fifth fret of the fourth string as a lead-in to A, and add E on the fifth fret of string 2 as a lead-in to D. Now you have two choices for the lead-in note to the root of each chord. Think ahead, naming the next chord in your mind, so you can mentally locate the target note and one of the correct lead-in notes for it.

You don't have to memorize or sightread the next example. Look it over and listen to the CD to get the idea, then flip the balance knob and try it for yourself. You may be only using four notes, but since you're deciding on the fly which lead-in note to use, you're improvising half the notes.

Track 4

## Targeting 3rds

Besides the root, each of these chords contains a 3rd and a 5th. All make good targets for soloing. So now let's use the 3rd of each chord, instead of the root, as new target notes. The 3rd of A is C♯, at the sixth fret of the third string. The 3rd of D is F♯, at the seventh fret of the second string. As before, try to nail these new notes right on beat 1 when the chord changes.

Track 5

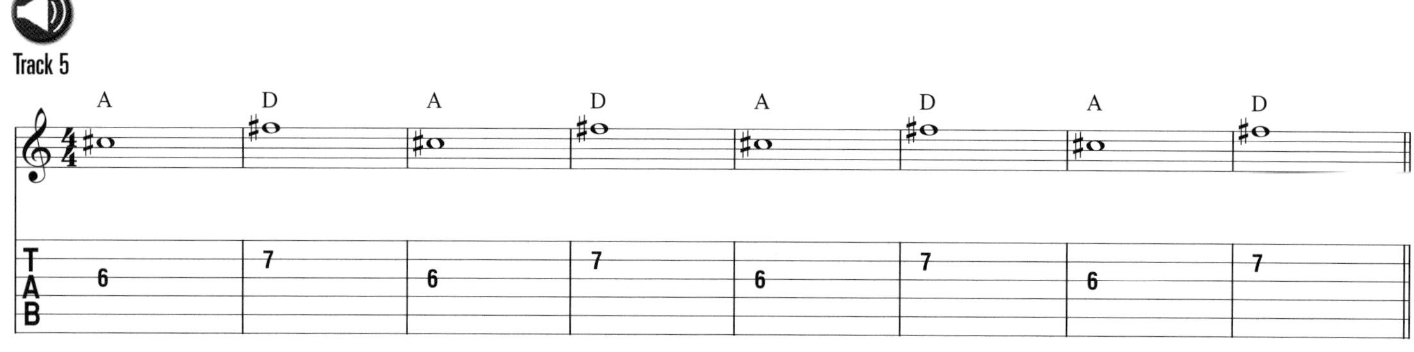


Our two possible lead-in notes for C♯ are C and D, both on the third string, one fret lower or higher than the target. Two lead-in notes for F♯ are E on the fifth fret of the second string, and G on the eighth fret of the second string. Now practice using one of the two correct lead-ins to the target notes: the 3rd of each chord.

Track 6

This idea of leading in (or *picking up*) to chord tones with consecutive pitches moving up or down is a central one in music. Many songs start with pickup notes or pickup phrases before the first "real" measure of music. I'm calling our phrases *lead-ins* because in its traditional definition a pickup does not have to move in consecutive (or *scalar*) order; it can be anything that is played before the downbeat. We're defining lead-ins, then, as pickup notes that move in a scalar fashion.

A sequence of notes will usually sound logical if it leads to a target note (a *resolution*) at the same time the chord changes. Controlling resolution (versus *tension*) is a goal we will gradually work toward. If you think about this, you'll see that I'm not saying that all good players hit chord tones all the time. They don't, and neither will you when we're finished. Too much resolution becomes overly predictable. Resolution is just an important skill we have to master so that we can do it at any time, then we'll move on.

We'll use the most basic of rock and blues scales for the next exercise: the A minor pentatonic scale.

**A minor pentatonic scale**

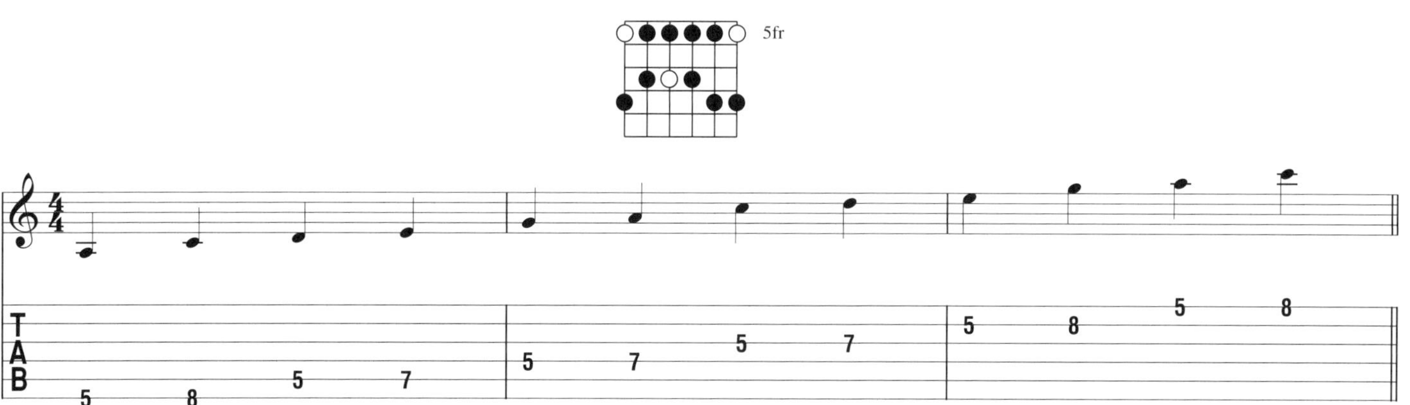


Review the scale pattern if it is unfamiliar. Notice that it contains the roots of both chords, but not the 3rds. Think about where the 3rd of A (C♯) and the 3rd of D (F♯) would fit into the picture as you practice the scale.

Now we'll use two consecutive notes as the lead-in, making it a pickup phrase, heightening the listener's sense of anticipation. You can think of the line of notes as an arrow flying through time to hit the bull's eye (the target note). To make a two-note pickup to C♯ using this scale, we can play A, then C, finishing the line of notes on C♯, which is on beat 1, as always. This means we have to start earlier, on beat 3.

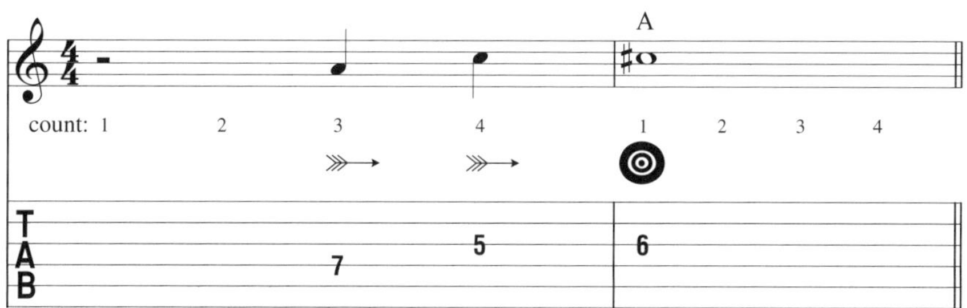

Here are some other possible two-note lead-ins to C♯. Play these starting on beat 3 as shown.

Consider some possible two-note lead-ins to F♯ (the 3rd of D) using the scale. Play these, again starting on beat 3 each time.

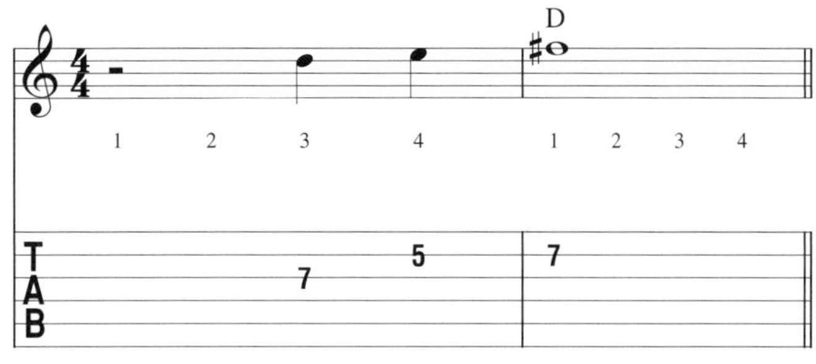

Now try leading in to both chords. First listen to the example, then mix out the lead guitar and improvise in a similar fashion. Make sure that you hit the correct target note on the downbeat, and the other notes come exclusively from the A minor pentatonic scale.

Track 7

Congratulations! You have just outlined a chord progression in an improvised solo. After an appropriate period of celebration, take the next step, which is mixing the two ideas. Target either the root or the 3rd.

## Eighth-Note Lead-Ins to Roots and 3rds

Now we'll start using *eighth notes*. Eighth notes are half as long (or twice as fast) as *quarter notes*, the notes we've been playing so far. We'll now use two eighth notes to lead in to the roots and 3rds of the chords. The lead-in will start on beat 4 of each measure. Look at this example, listen to the CD, and then improvise in a similar fashion.

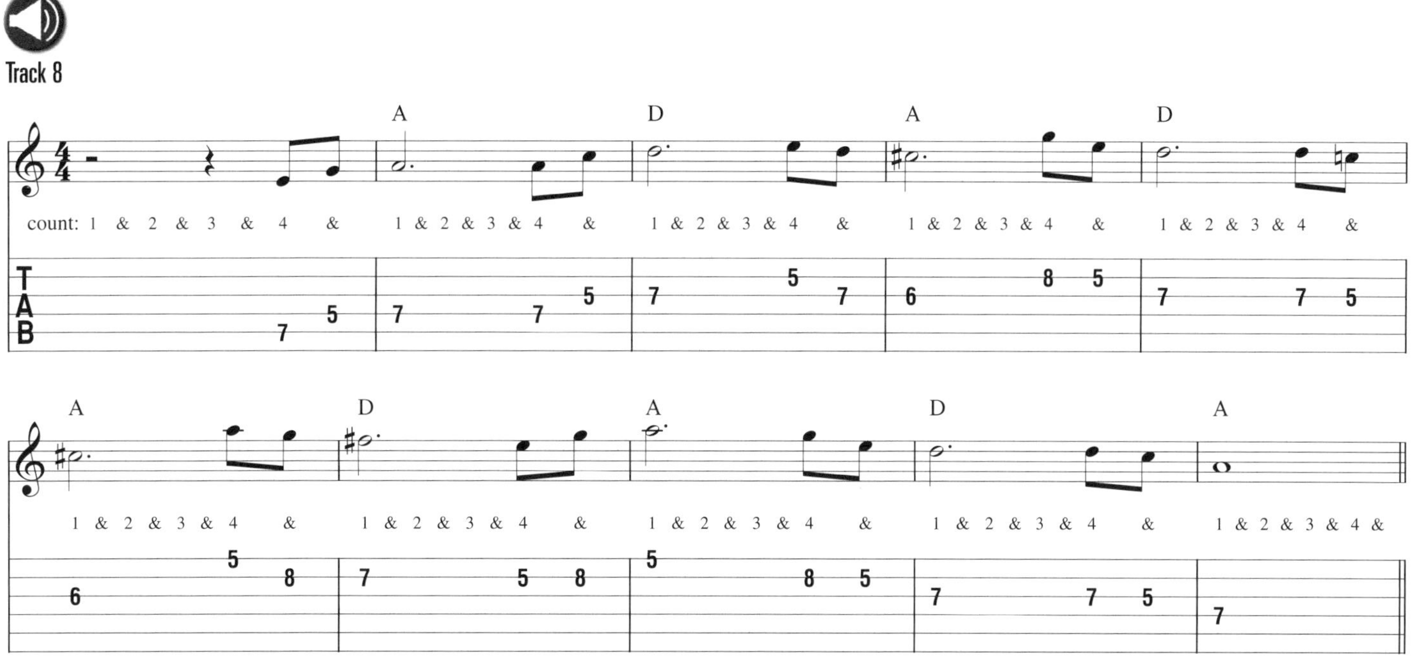


If you have trouble starting on beat 4, it's OK. This chapter is just part of a preview. In Part II, after setting up your practice schedule, the crucial skill of counting beats is the first thing we'll cover.

## Disguising the True Genius of Your System

The lead-in phrases we've used so far are not something I recommend you go out and play endlessly on a gig (although if applied with taste, they will sound good). They're really meant to train your reflexes to anticipate chord changes, rather than stand alone as licks. Right now the melodies we are creating sound a little bit obvious. To help that, we'll add some scale notes *after* the target. Add one or two notes only, so that you can keep in rhythm and come back with the lead-in on beat 4. Making the additional notes chord tones as well, as in measures 1 and 4, can sound quite musical.

# 2 Chord-Tone Targets on a Basic Blues

What we've played so far is sounding suspiciously like the blues. All that's needed is the familiar 12-bar structure and one more added chord: E. Use the E chord shape found at the seventh fret.

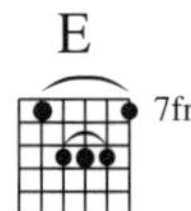


Be sure to memorize and practice the chords, shifting cleanly between them. The chords are played in whole notes with no extra rhythms to help you in targeting chord tones on time when soloing.

For this solo, don't move out of the fifth fret position at all. It's important that you keep your place on the fretboard. Keep your first finger at fret 5 for now. During the solo, when the E chord comes along, we'll target its root (E) at the fifth fret of the second string, and its 3rd (G♯) at the sixth fret of the fourth string.

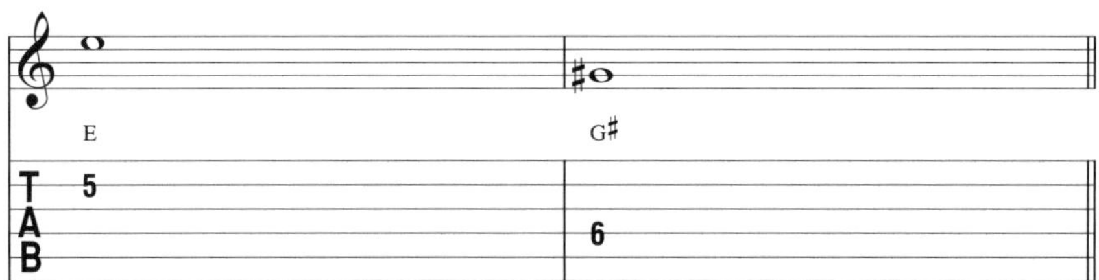


The 3rd of each chord determines its *quality* (major or minor) and is often the note that moves when the chords change. The presence of the 3rd also tends to imply the sound of the root for the listener. (In a band situation, the bass often supplies the root anyway.) By hitting the 3rds, we emphasize the sound of the chord movement.

## Hit the Targets

CD track 10 contains three choruses of the 12-bar blues progression. (A *chorus* means a repetition of the entire solo form. A bandleader may tell you to "take three choruses.") As a review of the progression and to help us get our bearings, the first recorded chorus of the solo is only targets played in whole notes (one note per measure).

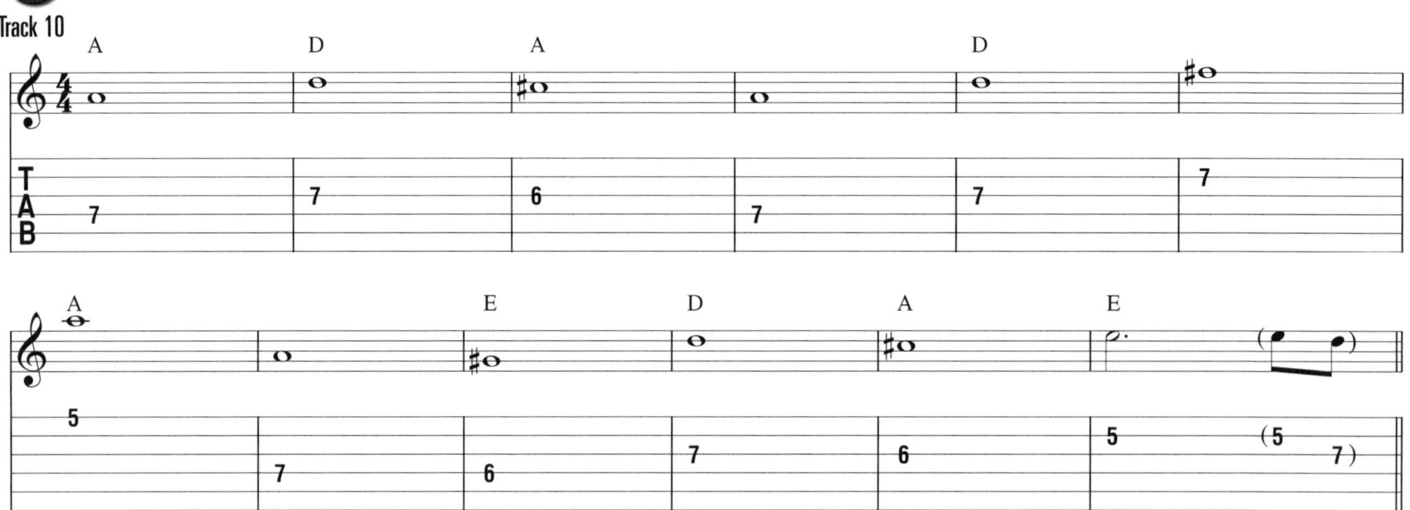

## Lead-Ins

The second chorus uses similar target notes while adding two-note lead-ins from the A minor pentatonic scale. Practice making similar approaches to the target notes.

## The Blue Note

Once we've established the sound of the chords with our target notes, we slip in a non-chord surprise by hitting the *blue note* in measure 6 (an E♭ is added to the A minor pentatonic scale, making it an A *blues scale*). You'll recognize this sound. It clashes with the D chord in a cool way, giving the solo a balance of nice *and* nasty.

Track 10 (cont.)

## Add-Ons

The third chorus elaborates on this approach by adding one or two notes after the target. Follow the spirit of the example. You get a little more freedom here, but don't allow it to distract you from your targets. Hit them all!

There is a standard blues ending on the last two measures of the third chorus. This variation in the chords sets up the feeling that the song is over. The chords change more quickly at this spot, so there is less time to think about the targets. Memorize what's written to play here.

Track 10 (cont.)

By trying the exercises in Part I, hopefully you heard that there is a musical logic to playing chord tones and a sense of momentum generated by leading into target tones at just the right time. We'll want these skills to become so automatic that the chords, while being accommodated, seem transparent to our overarching melodic intentions.

# Part II:

## A Solid Foundation

After those first couple of lessons, my students are lulled into a nice state of relaxed, easy confidence. They're thinking, "This is a piece of cake. We just jam on blues every week and he shows me a couple of new notes to throw in. I'll be headlining the Hollywood Bowl in no time." Only when we've reached that point do I start crushing vital organs.

Here in Part II we cover all the basics you'll need to learn the chord-tone soloing method in Part III. Depending on your starting level, it'll take from three months to a year of focused practice to get a decent grasp of the skills laid out here. This is normal, and you may proceed into Part III while you're still working on the stuff in Part II.

If you already have a strong background of theory applied to the guitar, along with the playing chops that come from years of organized practice and gigs, you may want to skim these chapters and proceed to Part III. Less wasted time is one of the benefits of self-directed study. But another benefit is that you can learn at your own pace, so maybe (if you have a thick skull like me) you should go over this part about 20 times! Even after playing and teaching for more years than I care to admit, I still need to review the basics sometimes.

The chords and scales in this book are the tip of a large iceberg. We're going to learn enough about them to solo over most progressions very effectively, but we won't be able to study every scale, arpeggio, and chord there is—especially the more advanced ones. For more practice with scales, arpeggios, and chords, and building them on the fretboard, you might want to check out my *Guitar Fretboard Workbook.* (No runny mess like with those other brands!)

# 3 Getting Serious About Practicing

I will mention lots of specifics, but a general rule of practicing is this: make it fun. Make it so you want to do it. If you start to hate practicing, you will not be a musician for long. Most of the practice guidelines I'll give have this idea behind them.

To get the most out of practice over the long term and still have immediate rewards (so you'll keep it up), you need to continually monitor yourself and the task at hand and steer for a balanced level of difficulty. You should always feel that what you are doing is a challenge, yet never so hard that you become frustrated. If it's too hard, slow it down and/or break the exercise into smaller pieces. If an assignment becomes relatively easy, increase the tempo or add a level of complexity in some other way (make the progression longer, articulate the notes with hammer-ons and pull-offs, etc.).

This idea of adaptive practice seems hardest for beginners to apply. They tend to become frustrated and keep slogging away in futility when something is difficult, rather than simplifying the assignment so they can get part of it and pick up the rest later. When something becomes easy, they tend to just repeat it without learning anything more, becoming bored in the process. Experienced practicers adapt their routines almost without thinking, continuing to practice variations on the same material until a solid and permanent familiarity is reached. Although you may prefer that your teacher tell you what to practice, you should at least learn to manage the pacing of your schedule yourself.

Do not consistently practice at a tempo beyond your capabilities. I'm often asked about this by players who want to build speed. It's OK to periodically attempt an exercise at a higher tempo than usual, to spur yourself forward. To avoid frustration, accept in advance that you will not be able to perform it correctly at this tempo. Don't continue to the point that you allow yourself to build sloppy technique. The majority of your time should be spent at tempos that allow you to develop the accuracy you desire.

To retain information and put it to use, you need consistent, effective, and efficient practice sessions. There are four main pieces of equipment you need to make them so: a metronome, a timer, a recording device, and a written practice schedule/log. It's also very helpful to have a solid music stand.

## Metronome

I don't like fancy metronomes because I take mine to every gig, eventually lose it, then have to buy another one. The simple type that runs on a 9V battery and has a single dial is fine. A nice feature of these is that you can turn off the click and play in time with the flashing light by itself for an extra challenge. I don't recommend the old-fashioned wind-up metronomes.

## Timer

The next requirement is a plain, old cooking timer with a bell or beeper, wind-up or digital. You can get one of these at any discount store for a few bucks. This is crucial, so don't slack off on me now. Get the timer!

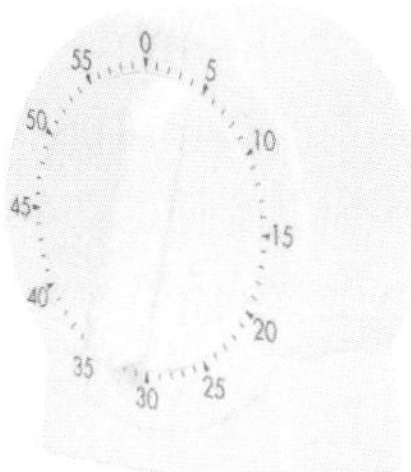


## Recorder

This can go from basic to extravagant, but whatever you use should be simple enough that it doesn't distract you from playing. You want to record and play back with just a few button touches. I accomplished most of my serious learning with a $25 tabletop cassette deck with a built-in microphone. It wasn't until much later that I acquired multitrack tape and then digital recording capability. This stuff is all great, and it does have valuable advantages (like allowing you to look at waveforms of your playing to see if the timing of note attacks is accurate), but you don't need it to learn how to play.

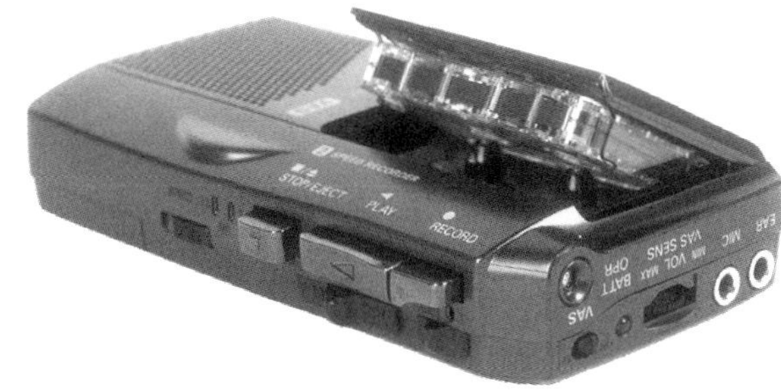


## The Practice Schedule and Log

On your written practice regimen, you'll make a list of things to practice, along with short time frames for how long you are going to work on them. You'll set the timer and only work on them for the specified amount of time, taking short breaks during which you'll clear your mind by thinking of something non-musical. When the overall time frame for the list is up, you will stop completely and do something else for at least an hour before you even think about doing the routine again. The overall time frame should be an hour or less per session for beginners. Experienced players can go longer. If you're not sure, go with a shorter session. This may not seem like enough, but we're talking about intense, focused practice sessions, thirty minutes of which are better for you than three hours of noodling around, mostly playing stuff you already know. A shorter daily time frame increases the odds you'll be able do it consistently for weeks, months, even years—and this is what you want. It's a marathon, not a sprint.

Don't get me wrong; it's great to play your instrument all day long, if it's what you want to do, and your life's circumstances allow it. However, that's not the same as this practice routine, during which you are constantly learning unfamiliar material. This you should keep short but never skip if you can possibly help it. If you are the type who likes to practice many hours per day, I still suggest keeping the routines in this book short and spending the rest of the time on other things like learning new songs or licks, transcription, reading, or composition.

Combine your list of things to do with a log of what happened during each session. You'll make a new one of these each week, modifying the new one to reflect things you wrote down during the week before. Don't make the schedule any longer than a week. A month of empty boxes ahead of you is intimidating, and a month of half-filled boxes behind you is depressing.

Each week is a new chance to start fresh, recommitting to the plan while adapting it to suit your needs and still maintaining the necessary continuity. A mistake I see students frequently make is learning something new and then moving on before practicing it enough to assimilate it into their playing. To prevent this, practice the same thing every day for two weeks or more. Then put it on review status, practicing it every two or three days, while adding new material to the everyday list.

Here's how a blank practice log might look at the beginning of the week. Rather than have me print one of these on every other page of this book, it's best if you examine this closely (everything on it is there for a reason), then customize your own version.

**Sample Practice Log**

| Date: | Monday 1/2/06 | Tuesday 1/3/06 | Wednesday 1/4/06 | Thursday 1/5/06 | Friday 1/6/06 | Saturday 1/7/06 | Sunday 1/8/06 |
|---|---|---|---|---|---|---|---|
| Review Major scales 2 min. | patt. 4 patt. 5 | patt. 1 patt. 2 | patt. 3 patt. 4 | patt. 1 patt. 2 | patt. 3 patt. 4 | patt. 5 patt. 1 | patt. 2 patt. 3 |
| Break 2 min. | Put | Guitar | Down! | | | | |
| Melodic 3rds maj. scale patt. 5 & 1 5 min. | | | | | | | |
| Break 2 min. | Put | Guitar | Down! | | | | |
| Major triad arp. patt. 4 2 min. | | | | | | | |
| Break 2 min. | Put | Guitar | Down! | | | | |
| Minor triad arp. patt. 4 2 min. | | | | | | | |
| Break 2 min. | Put | Guitar | Down! | | | | |
| Record rhythm track at new tempo 10 min. | | | | | | | |
| Break 2 min. | Put | Guitar | Down! | | | | |
| Arpeggiate progression 10 min. | | | | | | | |
| Break 2 min. | Put | Guitar | Down! | | | | |
| Target Roots & 3rds on prog. 10 min. | | | | | | | |

Total time: 53 minutes
Notes:
Stick to timer; write tempo and actual time spent.
Use metronome on all; record highest tempo at which exercise was accurately executed.
Be happy; maintain a positive attitude.

As each session moves along, you'll write the tempos and the actual time spent on each exercise in its respective box, along with any other reminders you want to make for yourself, like "use fourth finger," or "try 85 bpm tomorrow," etc.

Each week there should be an assessment, during which you celebrate every tiny bit of progress you may have made. If your boxes are not full, meaning you played but didn't use the schedule/log or skipped practice a day or two, don't beat yourself up over it. From a psychological standpoint it's better to emphasize all forms of *positive reinforcement* and avoid any *aversive stimuli* (like self-inflicted punishment), which doesn't really help and can have unintended negative effects. Positive reinforcement is the best way to sustain your practice habits. If there is a problem, consider ways to make the schedule easier to follow. One reason the schedule is only one week long is so that you can modify it regularly. I've been doing this for years, and it's rarely perfect. The fact that you use it at all is a step in the right direction, and it will get better over time.

You're dealing with a part of your brain that can only make decisions based on concrete stimuli. In a way your practice ego is like a child, to whom abstract and distant goals mean nothing. Treat it right, though, and it'll take you far. Which brings us to...

## Housebreaking the Ego

Habitual actions like daily practice and even the mechanical aspects of our playing are a function of the limbic system, which operates below the level of consciousness, also governing impulses, moods, and emotions. It's the same part of the brain that drives us to eat and sleep. It's much faster in operation than the part of the brain with which we consciously think, the neocortex. That's why we must practice in order to learn to play just about anything. (The neocortex conceives it, but the limbic system is responsible for doing it.) Obviously very powerful, it's also primitive, responding only to immediate motivation. The limbic system is quick to react but learns complex behaviors very slowly, and if we're not careful it can pick up exactly the opposite habit from what we want. By taking its nature into account we should be able to make it follow our will. Sometimes it needs to be tricked.

When we stop to think about it, we know we should practice. Why is it, then, that sometimes we don't want to?

Consider an untrained dog, snoozing by the fireplace. He shares (more or less) the same lower brain anatomy with us, without the burden of our highbrow neocortex. Faithful Fido will lie there enjoying his warm spot all day, until something—hunger, let's say—spurs him to move. Once motivated, he won't stop looking (or begging) for food until he gets it, and once he does he'll keep eating until the food is gone or he is so full he's about to explode. The same goes for everything else he does. He'll play until he is (or you are) exhausted and will try to continue a walk beyond the time you can spare for it. But if you are patient, firm, and consistent about teaching him, he can definitely be housebroken and learn to sit, heel, and fetch. Once he's learned these things, they're in his memory for good.

I'm no brain surgeon, so I could be full of beans with that little story. I definitely know that when it comes to practicing, it applies to me. I usually don't feel like practicing at first, but once I consciously force myself to start, I won't want to stop. I'll tend to continue until I am fried and my schedule is out the window. Continuing to practice in that condition is inefficient. We don't want that. Every minute should count for maximum progress.

Suppose you're learning a lick from somewhere—a book or magazine. You want to plant a clear image of it in your mind so you'll remember it. You take the time to go slowly through all the notes, one at a time, piecing it together. Just when you think you soon might be able to make some sense out of it—*ding*, there goes the timer. But you don't want to stop! You were just about to get it! The urge to keep going until you do get it is practically irresistible! And when you do get it, don't you want to then try to play it FASTER?! But you can't play it faster, because you just learned it. (Only the neocortex knows it.) The limbic brain gets wind of the knowledge and is all excited, but it needs more time to catch up. You should pack it in and work on the lick a little more tomorrow, but unfortunately this idea is one the limbic brain can't accept! Now you are repeatedly, till the wee hours of the morning, trying to do something that is impossible! Finally in utter exhaustion and disgust you throw your guitar down, saying, "This sucks. *I* suck. I'll never get this." Uh-oh. You just gave yourself an aversive stimulus.

Sometime the next day, you rise in a dignified manner (but perhaps at an undignified hour) and go about your life. The guitar is there but you pass it by; other things that need to be done seem to take on more significance. Practice time comes, but a tiny (though strong) feeling, not even really a voice, echoes, "This sucks. I suck. I'll never get this..." You remind yourself you need to practice, but you must do the dishes first. A TV show grabs your interest for a while. Then the phone rings; someone wants you to go out. Now you're in trouble. Your subconscious is telling you that practice sessions are a threat to your well-being, when there is fun to be had outside! It has no concept of time or organization; it doesn't know what a measly hour of delayed gratification is. It only responds to stimuli.

Now back the truck up! Imagine what happens if you take control at that one crucial time. You're just about to get an inkling of what this really cool lick is about, when—*ding*, there's that timer you wasted your money on. At that point you say, "I must have set that thing for a reason. I am running this program, not my urges." You put down your guitar. The next day, practice time can't come soon enough, and the first thought in your mind is, "Hey, what was that lick I was working on? I can't wait to check it out again."

The lesson here is that a good way to keep practicing is to always stop practicing on time. Besides the emotional reasons, we know that with multiple short exposures to a piece of information, retention is better than with an equivalent total time all in one sitting. Think about a telephone number that you dial once a day for thirty days, versus one you dial thirty times in one day and never again. Which number will you be more likely to remember later?

There are some good books on learning theory that you can apply to your practice; most of this is just common sense (which seems to disappear every time I pick up a guitar), already applied by every school or program that works. For instance, it's a good idea to introduce external forces to help you keep your practice schedule. Post your written practice schedule in a prominent place, like the refrigerator door (don't laugh, it works), where you know you'll see it. Let family and friends know what you are doing. They don't have to police you; the simple fact that you know others know can help you stick to it.

The limbic brain is responsible for feeling passionate about things. Suppose we could tap into the source of our drive to eat, seek a mate, and protect ourselves, and make it motivate us to practice. One way to do it is, ironically, to learn to play really well. This will in fact happen to you at some point. (Keep telling yourself!) Your own playing will satisfy you to the point that it becomes a positive reinforcement to practicing. The more you play, the better you get, and the more a part of you it will become. You'll feel something is missing if you can't practice.

# 4 Timing

In Part I we saw the value of hitting chord tones exactly when the chord sounds. Without good control of your timing, this can be hard. All of us realize at some point that we need work on this, and the best way to start is by counting, both along with recordings, and especially along with a metronome. The good news is that once a basic counting ability is acquired, the rest of the exercises in this book will tend to reinforce and refine it.

The first way to work on your timing is to count the beats aloud along with the music: "*One, Two, Three, Four, One, Two, Three, Four...*" Do it! Count aloud, four beats for each chord, along with CD tracks 2–10. I can't overstress the importance of learning to count in steady time, and learning to count while playing. You could play for years without learning to count and be only slightly better than when you started. Sorry, it's the truth. So, start now and keep working on counting every day until you can do it on demand.

**Practice Counting Away From the Instrument**

It's hard to learn two new things at once. So, if you are new to counting in time to music, practice counting along with tunes on the radio or a CD, without your instrument. The majority of popular songs are in 4/4 time, with the bass drum played on beats 1 and 3, and the snare drum on beats 2 and 4. Listen to music, count the beats aloud, and tap your foot on each beat. Do this throughout the day when you hear music: commercials, in elevators—anyplace. After a few weeks, counting in 4/4 time will seem pretty easy. Keep going. It needs to become second nature, always going on in the back of your mind while you play.

## Working With the Metronome

First, set the metronome at a slow tempo: 60 beats per minute (abbreviated *bpm*). If you are a right-handed player, tap the toe end of your right foot (not the heel) down on the floor with each click, and tap your right hand on your leg at the same time, so your foot and hand are moving together.

Obviously, in order to come down, your foot and hand have to come up, too. This upstroke needs to be evenly timed as well. Imagine that the top of your foot is hitting something when it comes up, like a little shelf about six inches off the floor. It should be timed exactly halfway between each downstroke. The click marks four quarter notes in 4/4 time. The hand and foot actually play eight eighth notes with their alternating movement. (The notes between the numbers are called the "ands" of each beat.)

Track 11

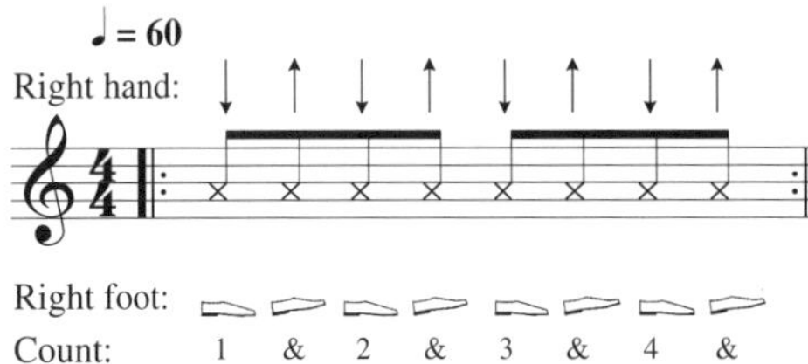


It also helps to imagine that there is a yardstick connecting your hand with the foot on the same side of your body. When the foot comes up, it forces your hand to move up. When the foot goes down, it pulls your hand down with it. Practice counting each eighth note aloud (*"One, AND, Two, AND, Three, AND, Four, AND"*) while moving your foot and your hand together. You need all these things happening at once: counting aloud, foot-tapping, and what will soon be picking or strumming. If this is your first time developing this kind of multi-part coordination (foot, hand, and mouth, in this case), be patient and practice it a little bit every day until it becomes easy to sustain for minutes at a time. The sore shins will go away soon.

Track 12

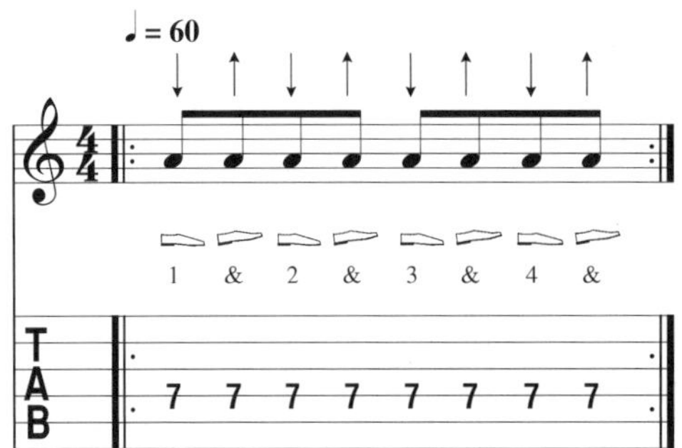


Practice your scales the same way—in eighth notes with the metronome—while counting aloud. Use *alternate picking*—the up-down motion from the foot-tapping exercise translates to picking direction. There are other picking methods people use (mostly because they want to play faster), but alternate picking is the best for learning to play with steady time.

At first, most people forget to keep counting as soon as the playing begins. And about half stop tapping their feet, with a majority of the rest going into spaz-foot mode. That's why we practice tapping and counting without the guitar at first, continuing for as long as necessary.

Glossing over this skill will cause nothing but problems, so don't allow yourself to stop counting and tapping your foot while you play, until you prove that you can:

- stop and resume tapping right with the beat at any time, no matter what you are playing.
- stop and resume counting aloud on the **correct beat number** at any time, as if you'd never stopped counting.

One of the primary goals of this book is to help you know by feel exactly which beat of which measure of music you are on at all times, no matter what crazy lick you may be playing. If I suddenly stop you in midsolo, you'll be able to say, "The last note I played was on the 'and' of beat 1, in measure 2 of a four-measure section of music." It may seem impossible now, but if you keep counting, you'll get there. It's really amazing that such a simple thing separates an amateur from a pro, but there it is.

## Staying in Time

If you have not worked with a metronome before, you may have a hard time locking in with it. Or maybe you start off okay, but then your notes drift away from the click until your playing is completely out of sync with it. Here are some ways to fix these problems. They're the perfect opportunity to try out your new daily practice schedule.

1. Alternate four beats of playing with four beats of rest, where you do nothing but listen to the click and tap your foot.
2. Go back to just tapping and counting without your instrument for a while.
3. Practice with an unplugged electric guitar so the click is louder than you.
4. Really listen to the click, even to the point of ignoring your own playing.

When you find yourself out of sync with the metronome, sometimes the only thing to do is stop playing and listen to it. That's OK; in fact, it's much better than continuing to play out of time. Stop playing, start tapping and counting aloud as soon as you feel the beat, then resume playing.

Use your body as a clock to help you lock in with the metronome. In addition to counting and tapping your foot, you can bob your head and rock your torso. Don't worry about how it looks; these are acceptable behaviors for musicians in any style. It'll make everyone think you're really "into" the groove—and you will be. You won't look like a fake, because you are doing it for a real reason: to help you keep the beat.

A good exercise is to switch the metronome to the flashing-light-only setting. Playing with it this way is harder than with the sound. Once you can stay with it, look away for a few beats, then look back and lock in with it again.

Finally (and this is a hard one), try setting the metronome at half the original tempo. If the metronome was at 92, set it at 46. Make these clicks the *backbeats* (beats 2 and 4) only. Start by saying, "*Two, four, two, four...*" along with the click. Then add "one" and "three" in between. When it's comfortable, start playing a little at a time.

## Why Is This Stupid Metronome Slowing Down?

It isn't. Most humans tend to *rush* (speed up) their playing at slow and medium tempos, and tend to *drag* (slow down) at faster tempos. Both can be bad, but rushing is the bigger problem for the less-experienced. When you rush, you play some or all of the notes too early—slightly before the next evenly spaced time division of the metronome. This is a big problem, because it makes the music sound tense, nervous, and amateurish, and can soon cause you to skip a beat, turning beat 4 into beat 1. Doing this in a band situation can cause a train wreck.

### To Stop Rushing

First, make sure you're not holding your breath as you play. It'll throw off your timing. If you find it hard to continue breathing normally while you play, it may help to integrate your breathing with your counting, inhaling on the same beat each time, like on the "and" of beat 3. You may also need to practice some easier music that contains some rests, during which you don't have to do anything but breathe.

Now, start playing with the metronome again, but let the click lead you; try to actually play after it. Drag as much as you can without falling behind the beat entirely. The idea is that your intentional drag will cancel out your natural tendency to rush, putting you right in the pocket.

Track 13

#### Intentional Dragging

Rushing is sometimes a byproduct of being nervous about what you are playing; the fear of missing a note makes you blurt it out too early. Repetitive practice at different tempos until you are relaxed and confident in your knowledge of a piece will obviously help, but it's harder to fix it when you are truly improvising, a situation where you don't always know what every note is going to be. Make sure that you practice improvising with a recorded metronome and chords alone, without a drum machine or sequenced groove to act as a crutch.

### To Stop Dragging

Since I want you to focus on playing slowly and deliberately for most of this book, dragging won't be as much of a problem as rushing, but when you pick up the tempos it'll need to be fixed, too.

Again, keep breathing normally. Try tapping your foot half as often, on beats 1 and 3 only. If a song's tempo is 208 beats per minute, set the metronome at 104, and tap your foot with the click, while continuing to play the song the same as before. Now the quarter notes you played at 208 are eighth notes at 104.

Then practice *pushing* the time. Play as far ahead of the click as you can without skipping a beat.

Track 14

### Intentional Rushing

Now you've practiced both ways: dragging and rushing on purpose, while still staying roughly with the click. The goal is to come down right on (the hip slang for it is *bury*) the click at any tempo. If there is variation, the preference in most styles of music is toward *laying back* (playing very slightly after the click while still keeping up with the overall tempo). Some exceptions are uptempo jazz, bluegrass, and rockabilly. You can feel the tension created in these styles by players intentionally pushing the time (but only slightly) to add to the excitement.

# 5 The Five Patterns

In Part I, we were provided with a head start; we were given notes to play and their exact positions on the fretboard, so that they'd fit the chords. Teaching ourselves to locate all the chord tones quickly so that they'll be under our fingers when we need them will require a strong understanding of the guitar fretboard. Luckily for us, minds greater than ours have already discovered the CAGED system. It is the key to locating any chords, scales, and arpeggios at all positions on the neck.

The five letters in "CAGED" stand for the five open-position (using as many open strings as possible) major chords. In the frames below, the roots of each chord are circled.

**The Five Chords of the CAGED System in Open Position**

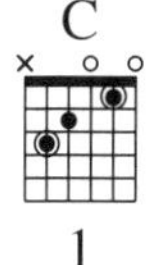


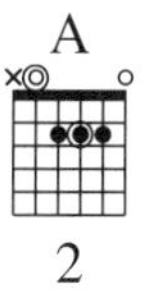

To avoid confusion, we're going to use the numbers 1 through 5 to name these shapes instead of the letters C–A–G–E–D. Using the numbers avoids confusion, because we can move any of these chord shapes up the neck. The letter name of the chord will then depend on the fretboard position of the shape, but the pattern number will stay the same.

For instance, here are the five patterns of the C major chord, in the different fingerings that must be used as you move up the neck. The notes in patterns 2–5 that were previously played with open strings must now be fingered on a fret. Follow the fret numbers given at the side of the chord frames. Don't get distracted by trying to play these chords perfectly right now, particularly patterns 3 and 5. Just satisfy yourself that each of these really is a C major chord, with the same notes (C–E–G) in every position.

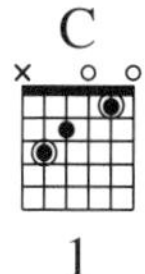


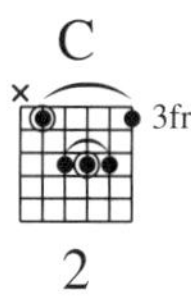


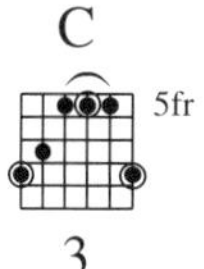


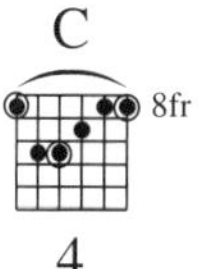


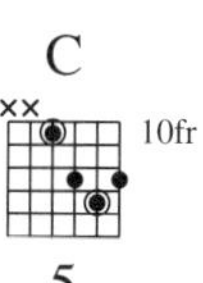


You can see how calling the second shape "C major, pattern 2" is a little bit clearer than "C major chord of the A shape." Using the numbers instead of letters is our only improvement to the venerable CAGED system. If you're used to the CAGED system already, then these numbers will enter your brain pretty easily: C–A–G–E–D = 1–2–3–4–5.

## Root Shapes

Even more important than these five movable chord shapes are the shapes created when you play only the roots of each chord.

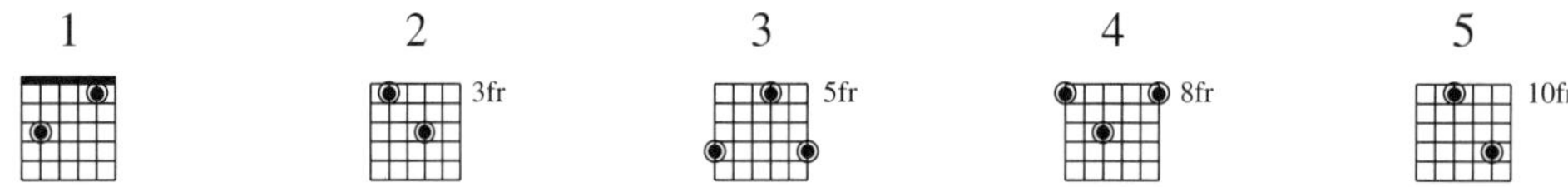


When overlapped end to end, the five patterns of *root shapes* show us every C note on the entire neck, ending and starting over with pattern 1 at the thirteenth fret.

**Root Shapes in C**

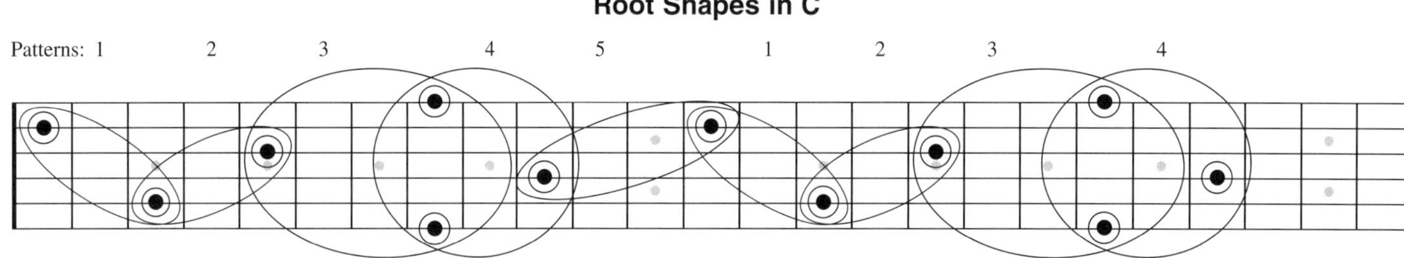


The pattern of root shapes is the same for any note. Here are the five root shapes for the note F.

**Root Shapes in F**

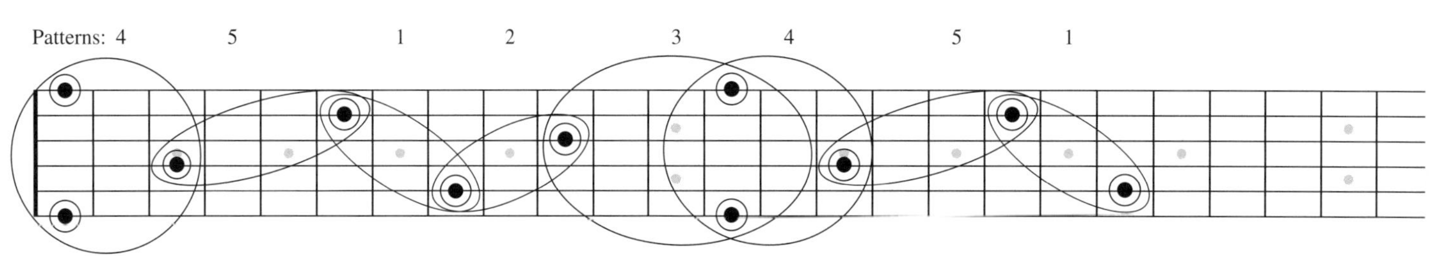


Make the root shapes the priority of your practice schedule. As soon as you can, learn to play them in any key, name them by number, as well as reproduce diagrams on paper from memory.

Every note, chord, scale, or anything else we can play is identifiable as being part of one or more of the five patterns. Of course, you could divide the neck up in any way you please and still figure it all out (maybe, eventually...), but this is the tried-and-true method.

### Diagram Exercise

On a blank sheet of paper, use a ruler to draw six-string, 24-fret horizontal fingerboard diagrams like the one above, placing six diagrams on the front and six on the back. On each diagram, draw the five patterns of root shapes. Move up by one fret each time: first all the Cs on the fretboard, then all the C♯s (equal to D♭s; label "accidental" notes with both their possible names), then all the Ds, then the D♯s/E♭s, and so on, until you finish by drawing every instance of the note B on the guitar. Label each root shape and outline it as in the example above.

# 6 Major Scales

Just learning how to play up and down major scales isn't much help to becoming a better soloist. You probably know some major scales already and may be wondering how to apply them. They don't sound very adventurous or exciting by themselves—maybe a bit like Christmas carols or hymns. Yet the pattern of notes they contain sounds completely different, depending on its mode of application and the underlying harmonic context, forming the foundation for every style of Western music, even the most extreme metal.

This pattern of notes is called the *major scale formula.* In order to learn the formula and put it to use, we number the notes in a scale from 1 to 7. There are two ways to learn the formula, and we'll need to remember both.

First, the major scale always contains the same order of *whole steps* (notes two frets apart when played on the same string) and *half steps* (notes one fret apart when played on the same string). (Whole steps and half steps can look different when moving from string to string, depending on the starting string. Such are the trials of a guitarist.)

**Major Scale Formula**

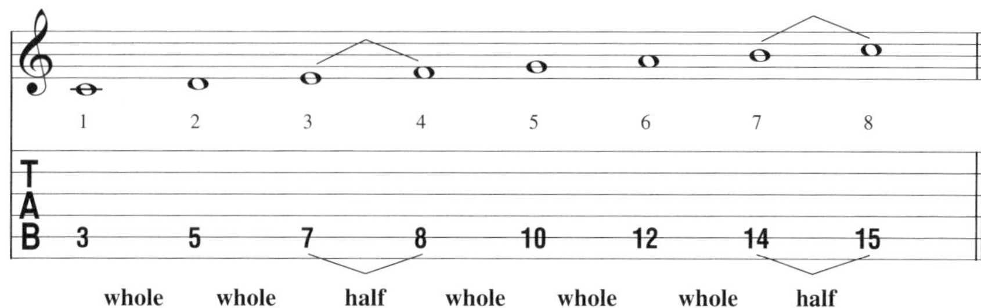


The other way is to just remember there are half steps from **3–4** and from **7–8**. I think this is the easier way to use the formula at first. When spelling a scale on paper, the half steps are marked with carets (^), and the lack of a mark between two notes implies a whole step.

**1 2 3^4 5 6 7^8**

Within each of the five patterns we learned in Chapter 5, we need to be able to identify every note by its number, 1 through 7, so that we'll know which ones are chord tones and which are non-chord tones. With five major scale patterns to learn, there are too many to be absorbed in one sitting, so let's start with pattern 1 of the D major scale.

**D Major Pattern 1**

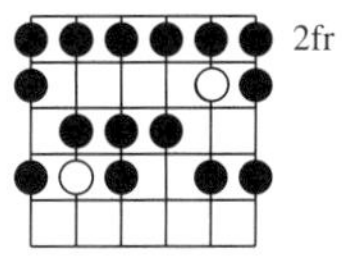


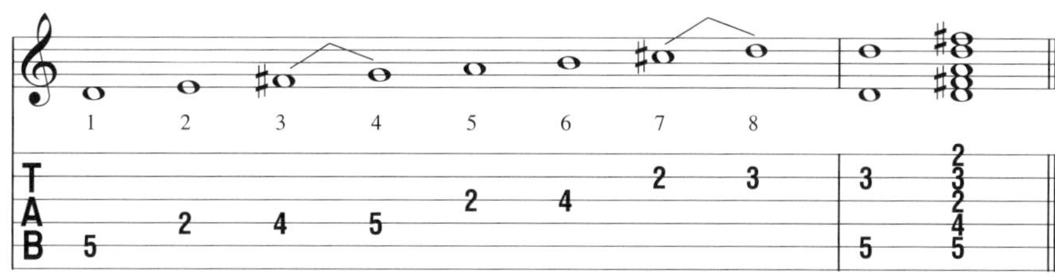

Recite the *scale degrees* (the numbers) aloud as you practice the scale. Notice the locations of the half steps from 3–4 and from 7–8. Follow up by reviewing the root shape, and finish by playing the chord shape: D, pattern 1. The scale, chord, and root shape should all be connected in your mind.

Add one of each of the five patterns of major scales to your schedule every two weeks, working on each one with the metronome until it is memorized. Use short, multiple time frames, as usual. Keep them on your schedule for several months (if this is new material for you), using the exercises in this chapter and the next. Many players keep them as the warm-up for their practice routine indefinitely.

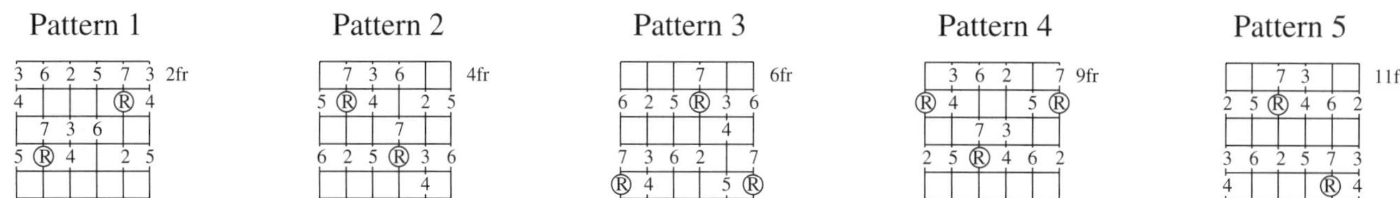


## Major-Scale Exercises

These exercises are *diatonic*, meaning they stay within one scale. To save space, any exercises that are self-explanatory are not demonstrated on the CD, but they still need to be practiced, in all keys, eventually using all five patterns. Each of these exercises, along with the others in later chapters, presents its own fingering problems that will help you develop clean technique. Strive for a *legato* sound—only one note sounding at a time, smoothly flowing from one note to the next, with no overlap or gaps between notes. Some players try not to use the same finger twice in a row when possible; others try to consistently use a finger-roll technique when there are two or more notes to be played on the same fret. Either way is valid; it's the sound that matters.

Descending through the scale is just as important as (and usually more musical than) ascending. First, practice starting the scales descending from the highest root in the pattern.

**D Major Pattern 1 Descending**

It's not enough to learn scales from the root. We should be able to start on any note. Start on a different scale degree each time and then descend as far as you can reach within the pattern.

D Major Descending From A, G, F♯, etc.

### Groups of Four

Make sure you understand and can play these; we'll be using them again. Start from the root and play four notes up the scale. Then start on the 2nd and play four notes up the scale. When you've gone as high as you can without shifting positions, reverse the order and descend.

♩ = 70

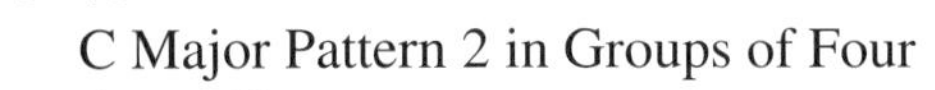

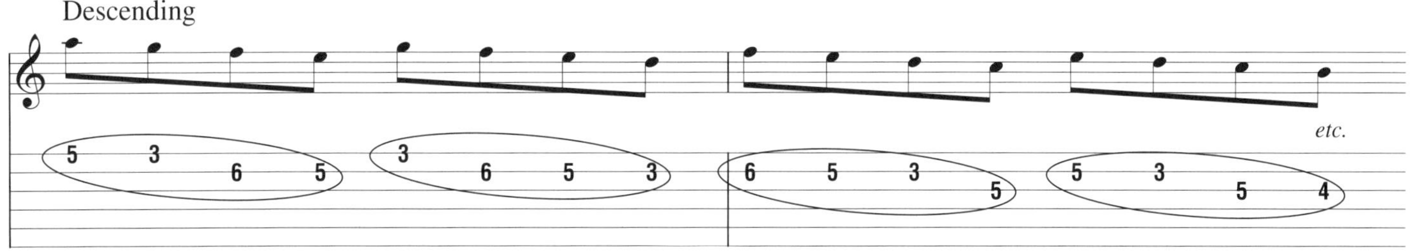


### Major-Scale Targeting Exercises

Eventually we need to know when and where to start a scale (or a piece of it) in order to land on a chord tone at the right time. To that end, the emphasis in the exercises that follow is placed on starting the scale in such a way that we feel target tones falling on the strong beats of the measure. The *strong beats* are 1 and 3.

Practicing scales with the intent to move toward these beats is an important form of ear training and critical for chord-tone soloing. Beats 2 and 4, the backbeats, are *weak beats* in comparison to 1 and 3. The weak beats, 2 and 4, are strong in comparison with all the "ands" falling in between beats 1 through 4; those are considered even weaker beats.

1 & 2 & 3 & 4 &
S w s w S w s w

Try using a *swing* feel when practicing these at medium tempos. In a swing feel, notes on each downbeat are longer. Notes on the upbeat are played later, and are therefore shorter. Swing is easier to hear than it is to explain. You can hear the slightly bouncy swing feel in the notes on CD tracks 16 and 17.

The "groups of four" exercise in the previous section does *not* resolve on strong beats. As a result, it sounds like the rather dull exercise that it is, with no real sense of movement. Following is the same exercise, but now it correctly resolves to the strong beats of the bar. Practice the major scale in groups of four, but starting on the "and" of beat 1. This helps develop the note-targeting reflex. By displacing the groups so they start one eighth note later, they now end on beats 1 or 3. Each group of four notes is a mini-solo, moving from tension on the starting note to resolution on the ending note.

Track 16

C Major Pattern 2, Groups of Four, Targeting Strong Beats

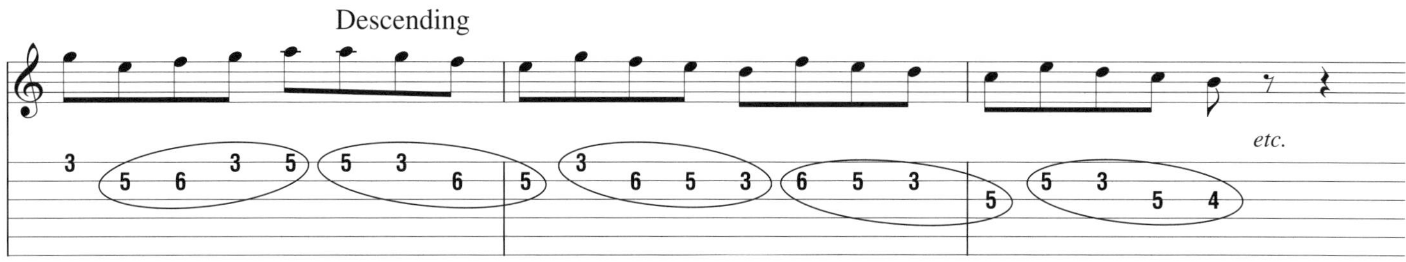


Practice descending groups of various lengths, moving up the scale, making sure that the final note of each group is on a strong beat. Count and rest until the correct starting beat.

Track 17

Descending Groups of Two, Targeting Strong Beats

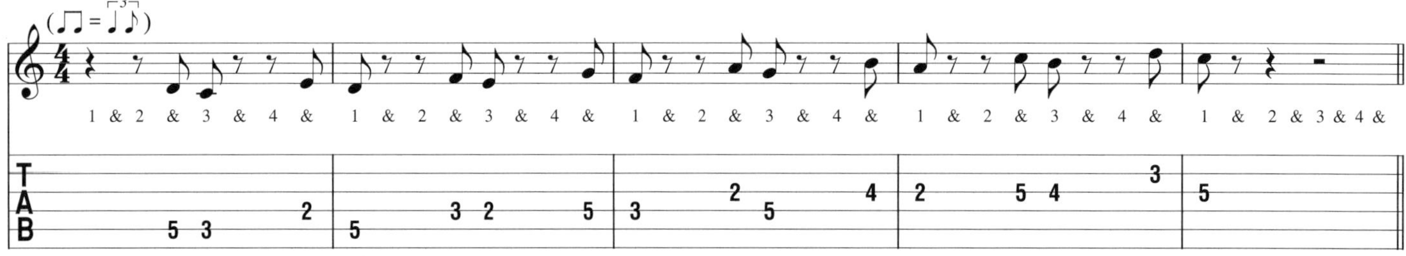

Descending Groups of Three, Targeting Strong Beats

Descending Groups of Four, Targeting Strong Beats

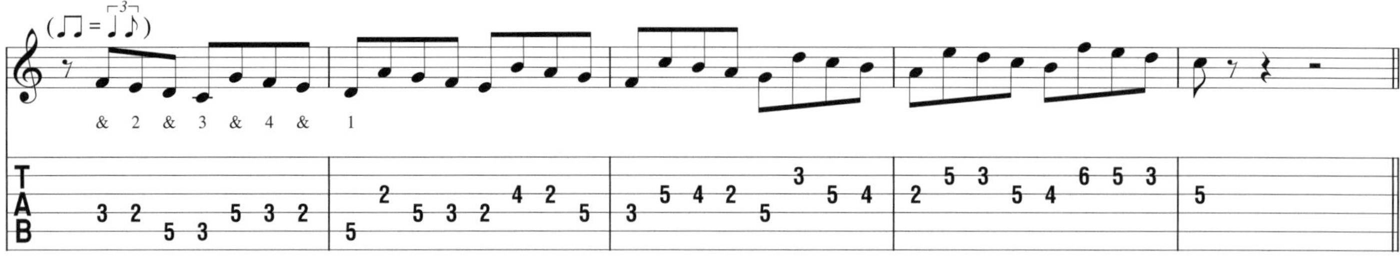

Descending Groups of Five, Targeting Strong Beats

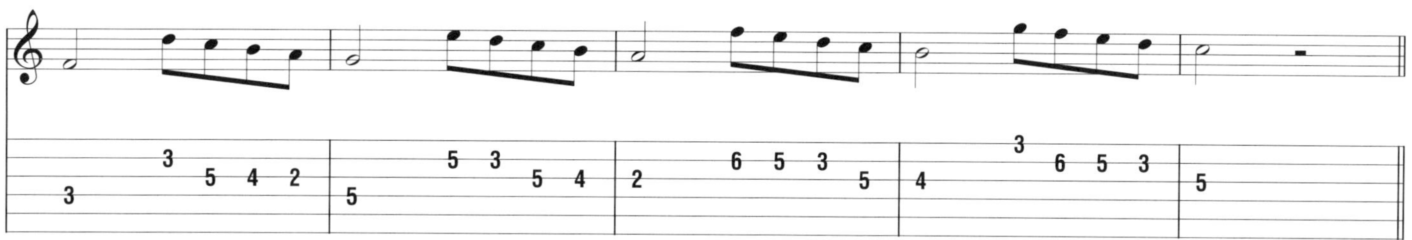

## Connecting Multiple Patterns

You can shift up to the next pattern (but stay in the same key) by adding extra notes on any string. Try to visualize the next pattern before you move into it. In this example we add one note to string 3, moving from pattern 2 up to pattern 3.

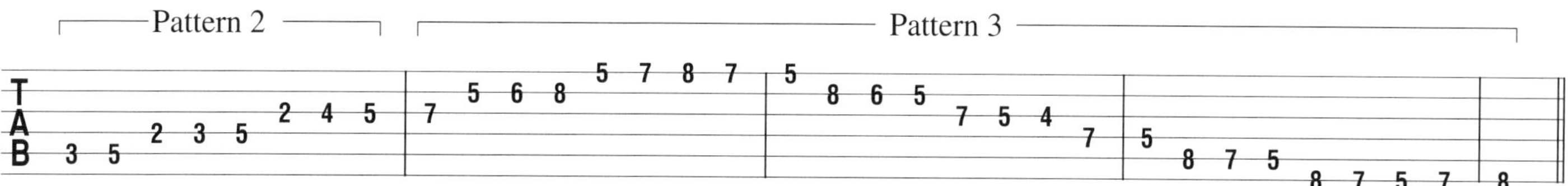


Practicing major scale exercises may not always be a lot of fun. Remind yourself that in order to play the way you really want to, just noodling around is not going to make it; you must practice the things on your list, in time with a metronome, with focus and discipline. Then, engineer your practice sessions so they're associated with rewards. Save the things you really enjoy most for after the strict regimen. Don't start the meal with dessert, in other words. Put the new songs, that new pedal, or anything else you're itching to do at the end of the session. For some, changing equipment and experimenting with new sounds is a way to keep motivated.

# 7 Intervals

An *interval* is the musical distance between two notes. If the notes are simultaneous, it's a *harmonic* interval; if they're at different times, it's a *melodic* interval.

The major scale is used as the reference for describing intervals. The interval number, or *quantity*, corresponds to a major scale degree. In addition, intervals have a *quality*. Intervals that match one of the degrees of the major scale are all either *major* or *perfect* in quality.

The intervals based on the 2nd, 3rd, 6th, and 7th scale degrees are **major** in **quality**:
major 2nd
major 3rd
major 6th
major 7th

The intervals based on the 1st, 4th, 5th, and 8th scale degrees are **perfect** in **quality**:
perfect unison
perfect 4th
perfect 5th
perfect octave

We can learn to identify these intervals by playing them from the root of the major scale shapes we learned in Chapter 6. In this example, we play all the major and perfect intervals from the root C in pattern 4, through two octaves. We'll eventually need to recognize the intervals starting from any string.

**Major and Perfect Intervals From the Roots in Pattern Four**

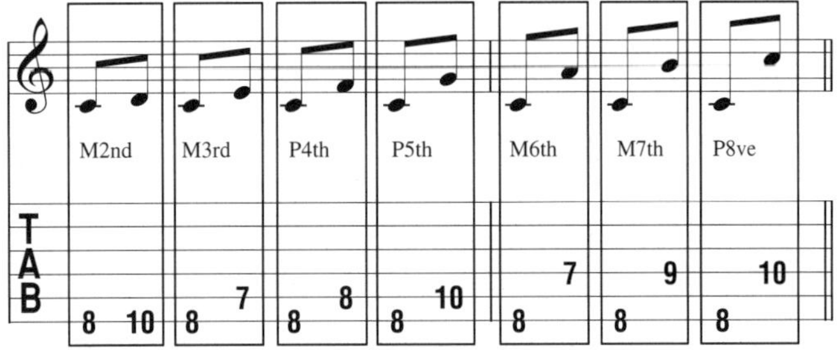


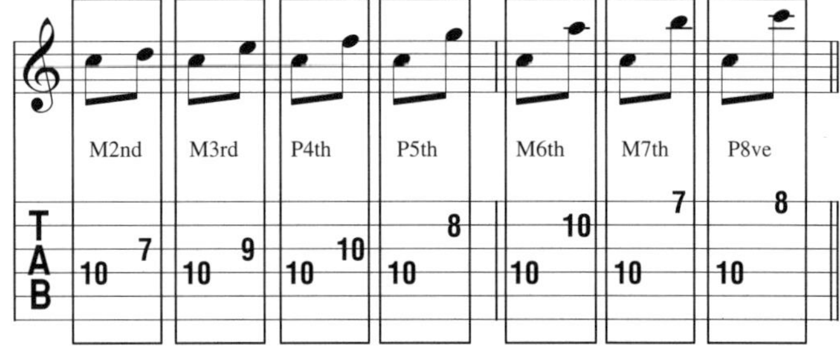


Relate intervals to the major scale patterns to help you identify and memorize them.

You'll notice by taking the exercise through the other four major scale patterns that there are multiple shapes in which intervals can appear, and the shapes vary a bit when they cross the second string because it is tuned differently from the others. Just as with learning the major scales, this complicates the job of learning the interval shapes.

*Diminution* is the decrease in quality of an interval. The opposite, *augmentation*, is the increase in quality of an interval. The intervals in the major scale may be diminished or augmented to give us names covering all possible intervals.

**How Interval Qualities May Change**

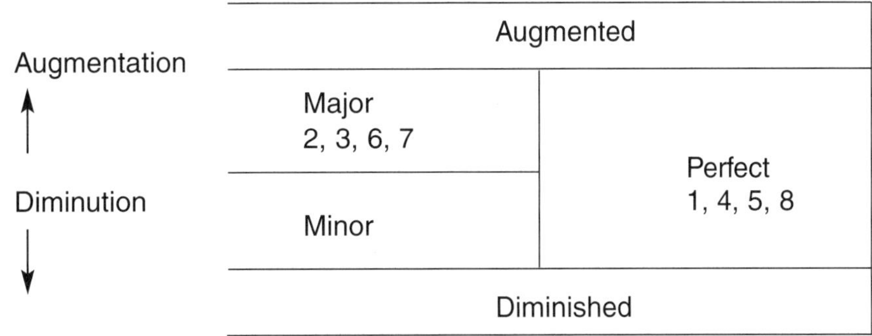


Major intervals may become first minor and then diminished, or they can get bumped up to augmented quality. Perfect intervals may only become diminished or augmented in quality. Because of this, there is no such thing as a "minor 5th," for instance.

Augmenting a diminished interval by a half step makes it minor or perfect, depending on which *quantity* of interval it is: one that must be strictly major (2, 3, 6, 7) or one that must be perfect (1, 4, 5, 8).

As shorthand terminology, both minor and diminished intervals are often simply referred to as *flat* and marked with the flat symbol only (i.e., a minor 3rd is called a ♭3, a diminished 5th is called a ♭5). Likewise, augmented intervals are simply referred to as *sharp*: ♯4 for augmented 4th, etc. Major and perfect intervals are implied by the lack of any qualitative modifier: a perfect 5th is just called a 5th.

The ♭5th/♯4th interval has an extra name: the *tritone*, from the fact that it is equal to three whole steps. The unstable sound (tension) of this interval is put to good use, making music move (toward resolution).

## Diatonic Interval Studies

Besides measuring from the root to each note, we need to know the intervals between the various notes within a scale. For example, the distance from the second to the fourth note in a major scale is a minor 3rd. We can confirm this by adding the whole step from 2–3 and the half step from 3–4. Because both notes are in the major scale, the interval is *diatonic*.

When we follow each note with one that is a diatonic 3rd higher, we get an *interval study*, something to practice to develop our ears and our playing technique. Studies like this may be based on any interval or even a series of intervals moving through the scale (e.g., a sequence of alternating 3rds and 4ths). The topic of interval studies alone could fill a book, but we'll stick with the basics for now: melodic 3rd sequences, and harmonized 3rds and 6ths.

First learn to play melodic 3rds moving through pattern 4, and eventually apply them to each pattern. This exercise is vital for breaking up scalar passages, teaching your fingers to skip around of their own accord. Notice that the location of the half steps in the scale creates major 3rds on steps 1, 4, and 5, and minor 3rds on steps 2, 3, 6, and 7.

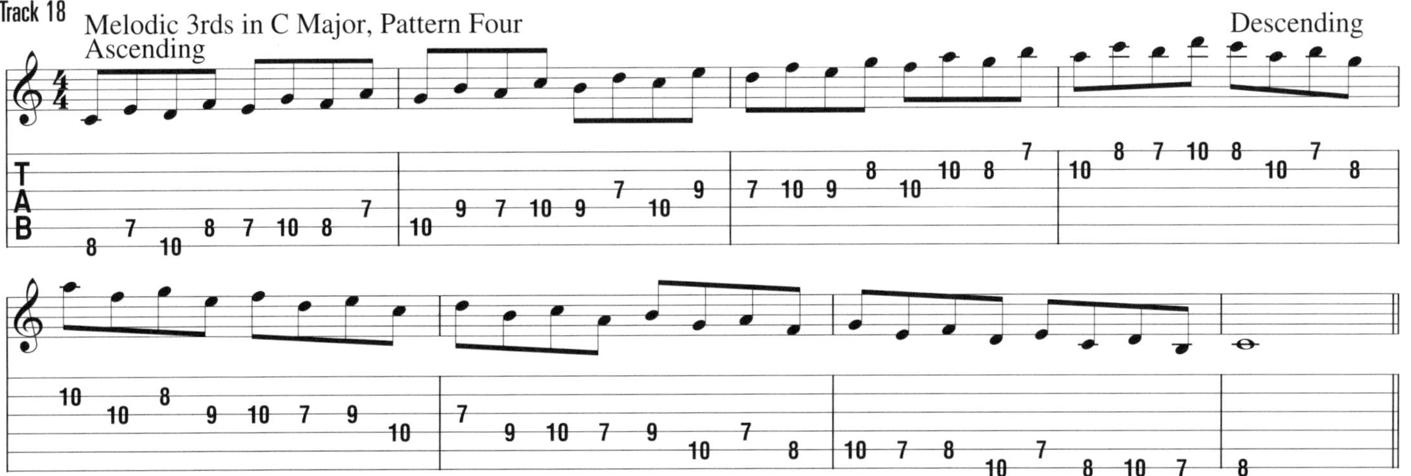

Next we have some harmonized 3rds, which are great for both rhythm guitar and soloing in every style. The easiest way to start learning these is to stay on the same two strings and move up or down the fretboard. Again, we have major 3rds on steps 1, 4, and 5, while 2, 3, 6, and 7 are minor. This example is on strings 3 and 2; you should work them out on the other string sets, and within each of the 5 patterns, ascending and descending, as a long-term goal.

Track 19

**Harmonized 3rds in C Major**

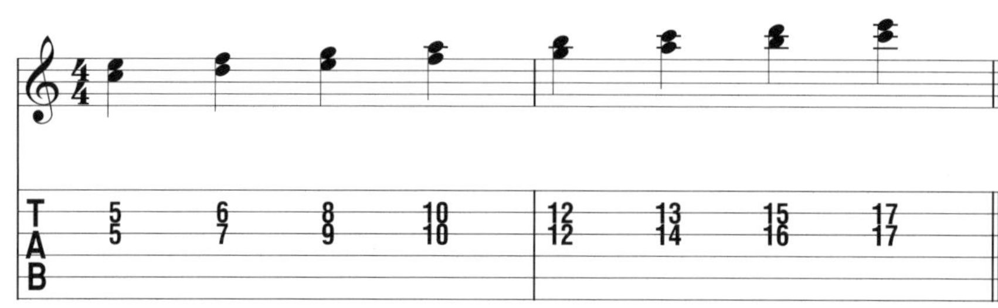


Also important (and fun to play) are the harmonized 6th intervals. Notice they contain the same notes as the 3rds, only the higher note is now an octave lower.

Track 20

**Harmonized 6ths in C Major**

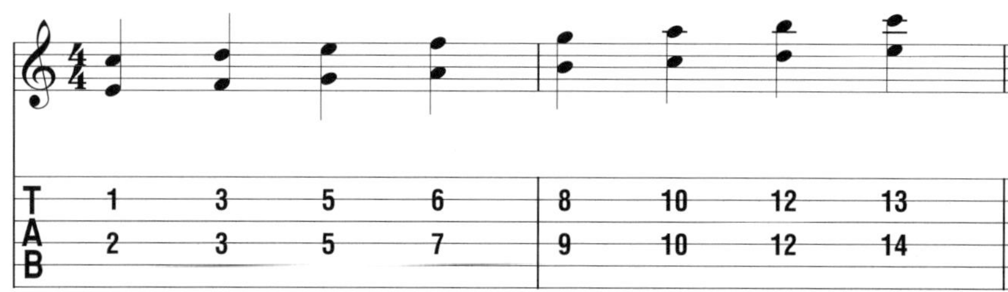


Diatonic 3rds and 6ths are *complements*: they add up to an octave, and are *inversions* of each other (C–E vs. E–C).

# 8 Chords and Arpeggios

An *arpeggio* is the notes of a chord played one at a time. We can think of chords and "arps" interchangeably when we study harmony. For instance, horn players can only spell out the notes of a chord by arpeggiating it, but they still think in terms of the chords in a tune when soloing.

Triad arpeggios are used in all types of music, applied directly over their corresponding chords in the roots styles, and also as *melodic substitutes* over various chords in modern pop, R&B, and jazz. Triads are the meat and potatoes in chord-tone soloing.

## Major Triads

The chords we used to examine the CAGED system are triads, chords that consist of only three unique notes, though on the guitar we often duplicate some of them for convenient strumming (or maybe just because we like being loud).

Just like the chords, major-triad arpeggios contain only roots, 3rds, and 5ths. These are the same as scale degrees 1, 3, and 5 of the major scale. When you practice an arpeggio, review the scale pattern and chord shape in the same fretboard position. Sometimes the chord and arpeggio shape with the same pattern number will cover slightly different neck areas from each other because of the nature of the instrument. This is because in a chord you cannot play more than one note per string, though you may do this in an arpeggio.

Below are the five patterns of major-triad arpeggios, written out for your convenience in the key of D (instead of C) to avoid any open-string confusion about pattern 1. Look for the five chord shapes of the CAGED system within the arpeggios.

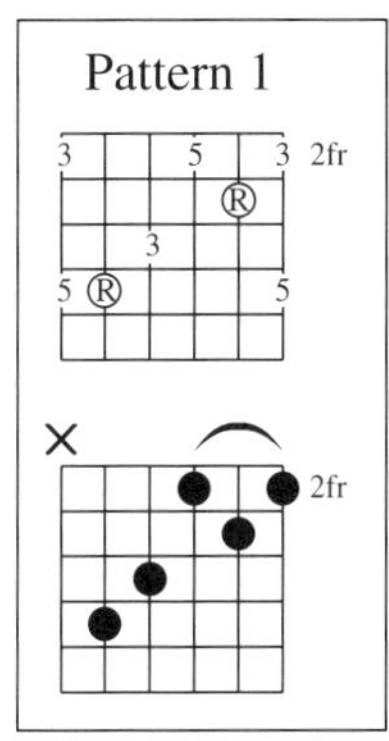


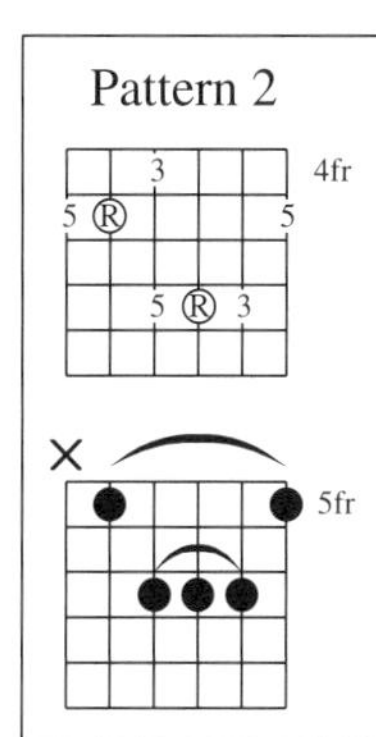


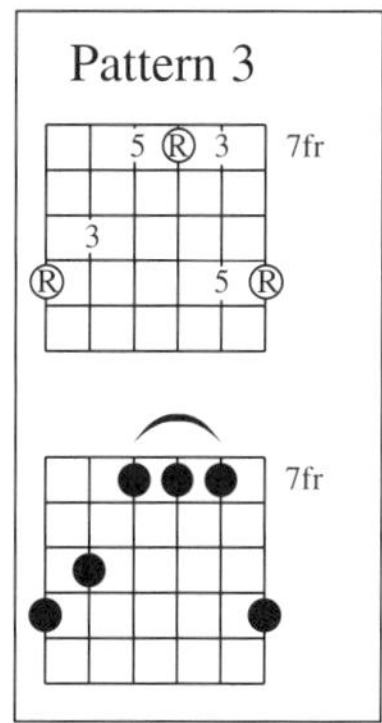


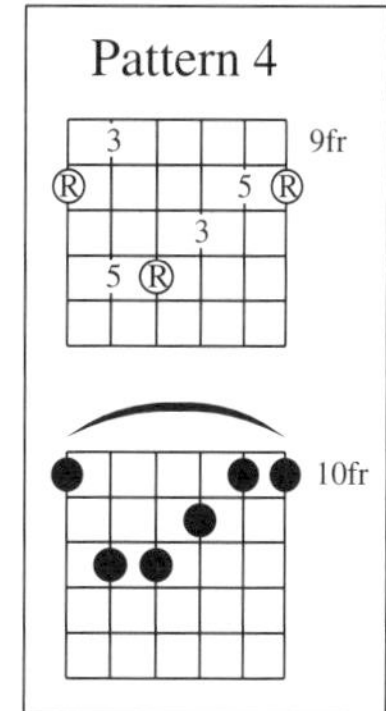


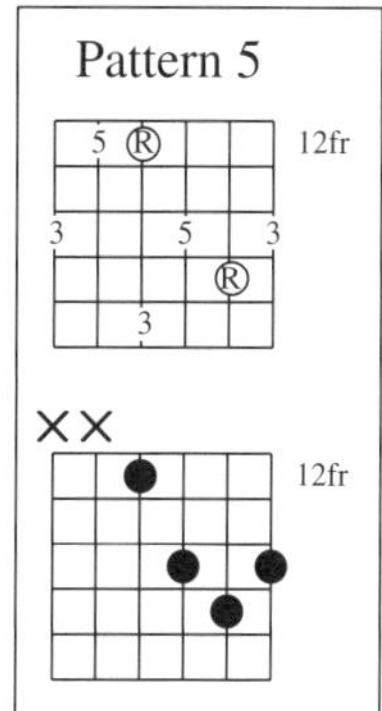


### Diagram Exercise

Make copies of the major-arpeggio diagrams on a separate sheet of paper (or even just in the margins of the book) to help you memorize the shapes with their numbers. Don't just lunge in and start playing after glancing at the page for a few seconds. Recreate the diagram yourself by drawing all the roots, 3rds, and 5ths from one of the major scale patterns (1 through 5) before playing the arpeggio. You want to plant a clear image of the arpeggio shapes in your mind, one at a time, relating them to the underlying major scale patterns and chord shapes.

**Playing Exercise**

Only look at the diagrams before or after playing. If you get lost, stop playing and look at the book. Get the idea? I don't want you playing and looking at the book at the same time! Tap your foot and play the major-triad arpeggios. On the CD, they're demonstrated in eighth notes at a tempo of 70 bpm (fairly slow), but I suggest a beginner start even slower—set a metronome at 60 bpm and play in quarter notes or half notes, if necessary.

On the CD, the five patterns of major-triad arpeggios are demonstrated in one key, but you should practice them in all twelve keys. When practicing these, or any shapes in the book, first start from the root and play up to the highest note in the pattern. Then descend to the lowest note in the pattern that you can reach without shifting positions. Finally, ascend back to the root, where you started. Once you feel comfortable with this approach, try starting (and changing direction) on any of the other notes, which is more of a real-life musical application. Maintain awareness of the root shape and the associated chord and scale pattern.

Having trouble remembering shapes? Try **blabbing** them. Recite the location of the notes in each arpeggio, like this:
"D major-triad arpeggio, pattern 1. Root, D on the fifth string, fifth fret. 3rd, F♯ on the fourth string, fourth fret. 5th, A on the second fret of the 3rd string. Another root, D on the 3rd fret of the second string. 3rd, F♯ on the second fret of the first string. 5th, A on the fifth fret of the first string."

## Minor Triads

Minor triads have a root, minor 3rd, and a perfect 5th. Here are the five patterns of minor-triad arpeggios and their associated chord shapes, which you should practice at the same time. Some of the chords may be unfamiliar to you, but you can see how these are derived from the arpeggio shapes, constrained by the limitations of strings and fingers. Any combination of notes that includes the root, ♭3, and 5 is a minor triad.

Since we're going to learn the arpeggios in all twelve keys, we can start anywhere. Let's start with pattern 4 of the G minor triad at the third fret.

Track 22

### G Minor Triad Arpeggios

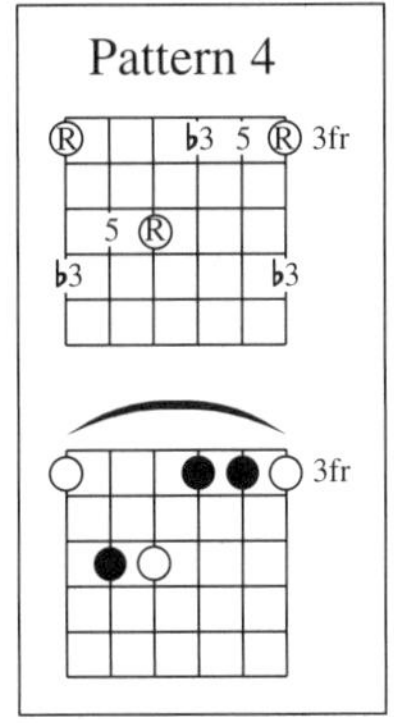


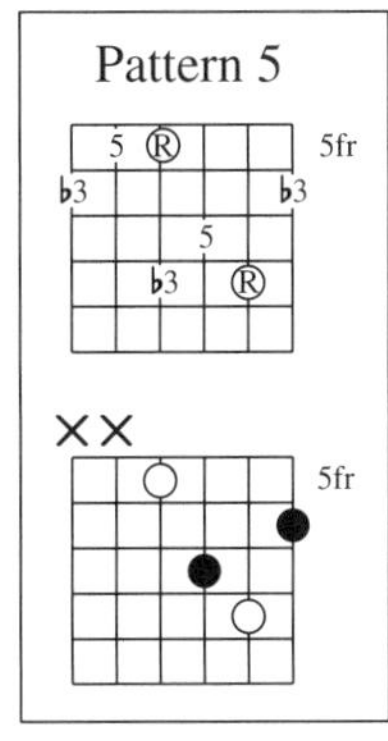


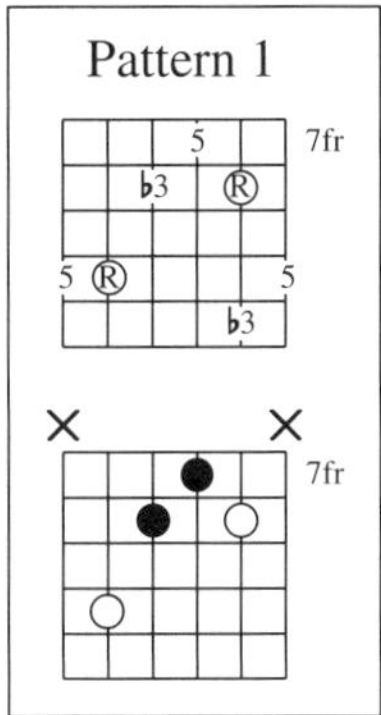


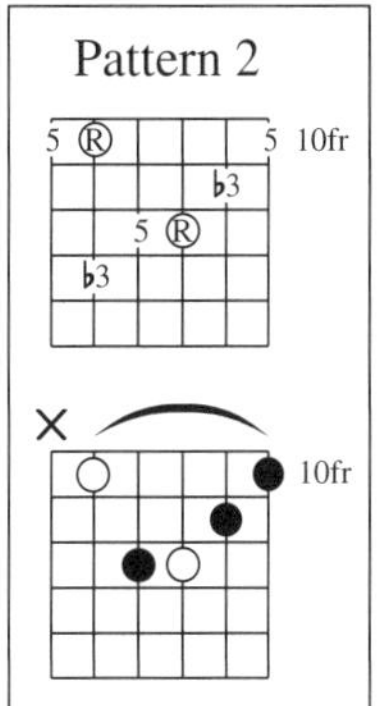


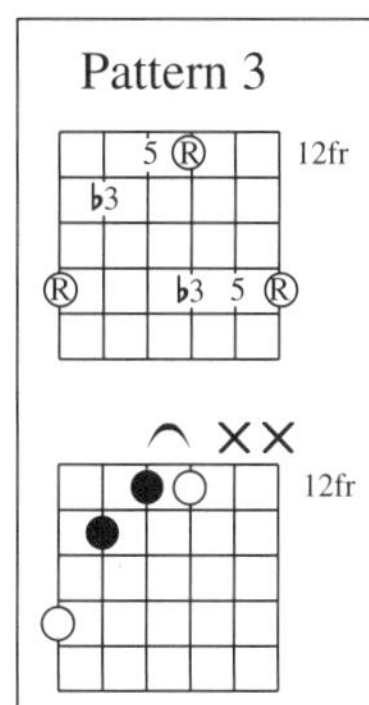


### Blab and Diagram Exercise

Look at each minor arpeggio and describe the locations of all its notes with the "blab" method I mentioned: "G minor triad, pattern 4, root on the sixth string, third fret. Minor 3rd on the sixth string, sixth fret, etc." Make your own diagram of what you are describing. Do this for all five patterns of minor arpeggios.

### Playing Exercise

First play the five patterns of G minor arpeggios. Then change to C minor: with a metronome set at 60 beats per minute, tap your foot and play the five patterns of minor-triad arpeggios in quarter notes, starting with pattern 2 of C minor at the third fret. Then do the same thing with all five F minor arpeggios, starting with pattern 4 at the first fret. Don't look at the book while you're playing.

By repeated playing of the five minor-triad arpeggios, you'll see how each one relates to the major arpeggio in the same position. The roots and 5ths are the same; it's just the 3rd that changes. We need to know this difference well, so practice patterns 1–5 of major arpeggios, with each immediately followed by the minor arpeggio in the same position.

## Diminished Triads

Diminished triads have a root, a minor 3rd, and a diminished 5th. Notice that each has two consecutive minor 3rds: from 1 to ♭3, and then from ♭3 to ♭5. Visualize the underlying root shapes and the minor 3rd intervals, looking for repeating fretboard patterns to help you find these chords and arpeggios, because they're not very easily related to the intervals of the major scale. Once you understand their theoretical construction, work on your own variations of the shapes given here. There are lots of possible ways to play these up and down the neck.

### D Diminished Triad Arpeggios

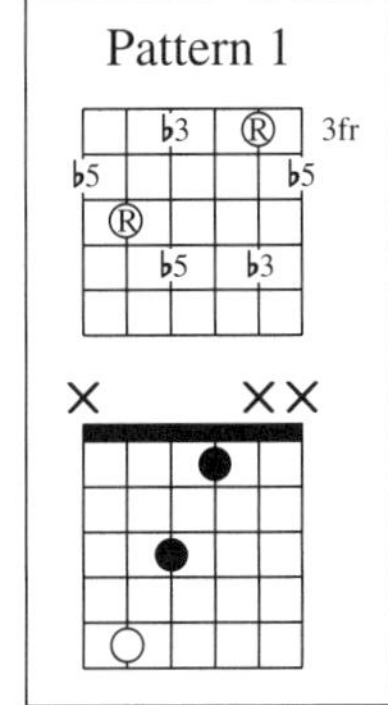


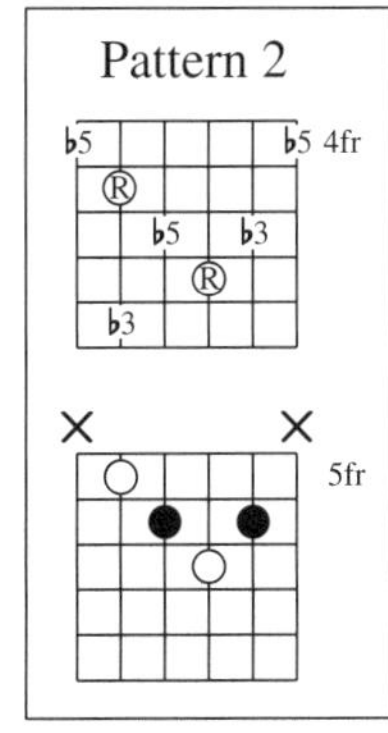


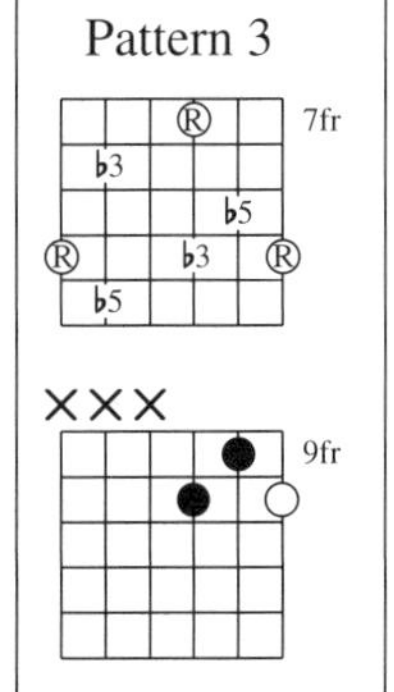


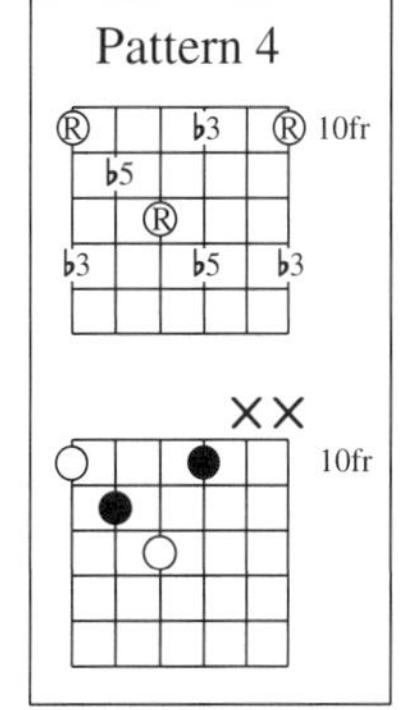


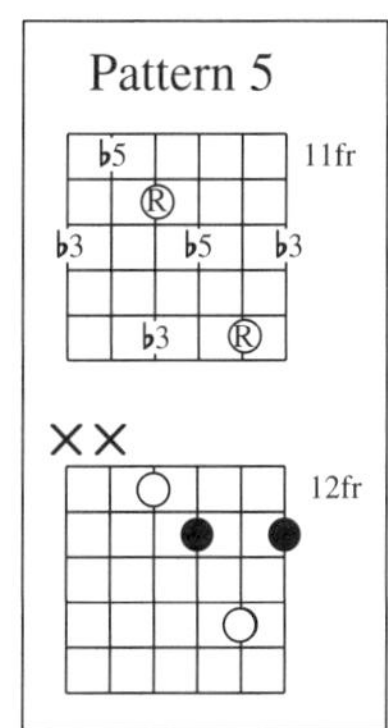


Practice each minor triad, then immediately follow it with the diminished triad from the same root. Recognize the one-note difference separating minor from diminished.

## Augmented Triads

Augmented triads are completely symmetrical, consisting only of consecutive major 3rds; the spelling is root, major 3rd, augmented 5th. (From the augmented 5th up to the next root is also a major 3rd.) Because of this, the shapes repeat every four frets, and any note of an augmented triad shape can be considered a root. When you are looking for an augmented triad, you only have to find one correct note and just fill in the rest of the shape. The chord symbol for augment consists of a "+" symbol added to a major chord. For example, the symbol for C augmented is simply C+.

### A Augmented Triad Arpeggios

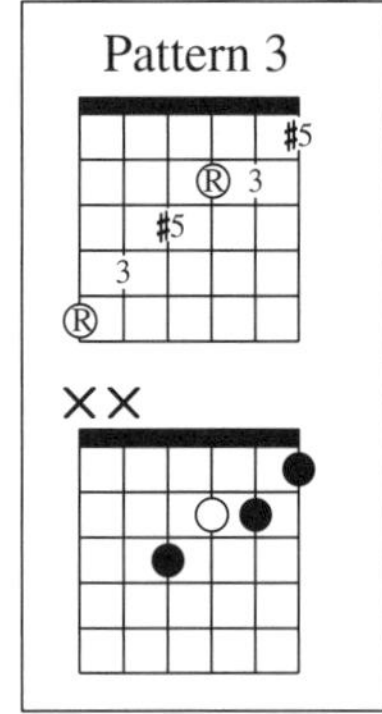


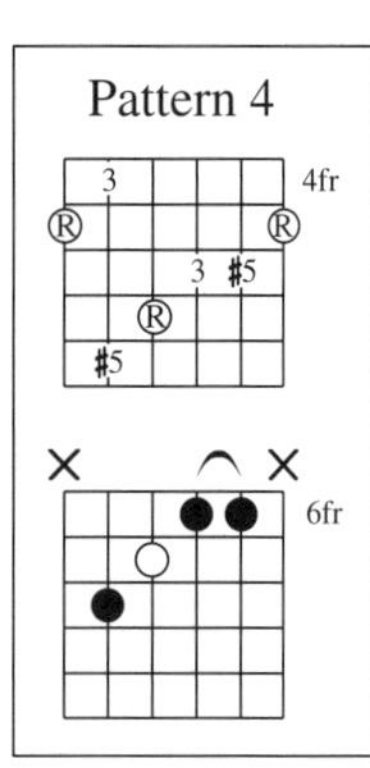


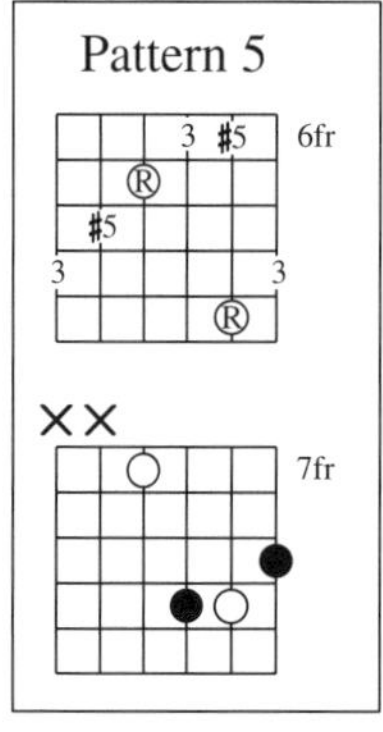


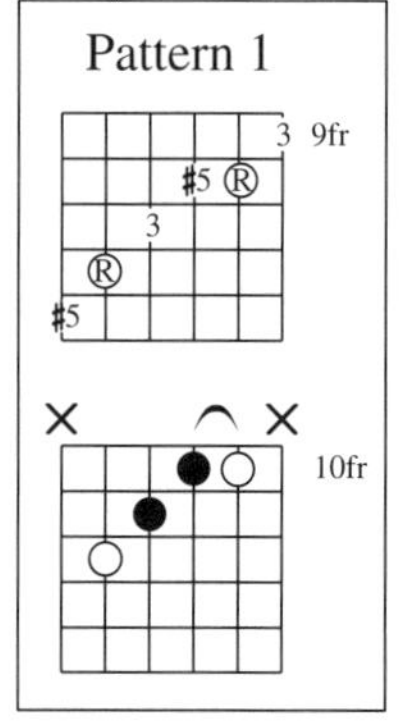


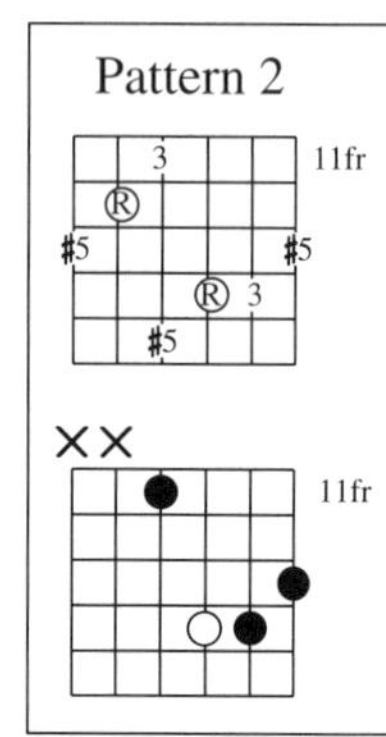


Practice augmented triads by first playing a major triad, then raising its 5th. As strange as they may sound when practiced in isolation, augmented chords fit perfectly in music when a feeling of tension is required. They also work nicely in a chordal sequence, such as C, C+, C6, etc.

### Compound Intervals

To make things clear in the descriptions of the exercises to follow, instead of the number **1**, sometimes I'll refer to the root with the number **8** when an ascending exercise crosses over into the next octave. In fact, throughout this book, when the examples span large ranges, all of the scale step numbers 2 through 7 may be referred to in the higher octave as the 9th, 10th, 11th, and so on, up to the 15th, if it helps show exactly what the notes are in relation to each other.

| 1 | 2 | 3 | 4 | 5 | 6 | 7 | 8 | 9 | 10 | 11 | 12 | 13 | 14 | 15 |
|---|---|---|---|---|---|---|---|---|---|---|---|---|---|---|
| C | D | E | F | G | A | B | C | D | E | F | G | A | B | C |

Conversely, for the sake of simplicity, high-numbered notes may be reduced by seven, making a "**9**" into a "**2**" again (even though it may be technically the wrong name for the note if there's a chord being played beneath it), whenever a pattern is not crossing into the next lower octave. This may all seem like excessive and unnecessary explanation, but in real life, musicians refer to these notes interchangeably all the time, so we need to get used to it. When an interval spans an octave like this, it is called a *compound interval.* The compound interval and its simple interval equivalent are always separated by seven: 2+7=9, 3+7=10, etc.

## Triad Arpeggio Exercises

We need to drill arpeggios to the point where they are applicable "on the fly" in soloing, so there are lots of exercises here, gradually increasing in difficulty, to help you learn them. Customize your practice schedule to track your progress. Stick with one exercise for several weeks, keeping your practice schedule short and balanced between easy and hard, as always. Move up just enough to keep yourself challenged, but not frustrated.

Besides helping you memorize the arpeggio shapes, these exercises contain melodic structures that you can use when creating soloing phrases. Each presents its own technical problems, and working through them will prepare your fingers for future gymnastics. Still, it's important to remember they're exercises and not an end unto themselves. Do your homework and put in the time on them to help you get where you need to go, but don't stop here.

### Arpeggios in Groups of Three

Play in triplets (three notes per click of the metronome). Each group starts one note higher than the last: 1–3–5, 3–5–8, 5–8–10. When you've played the highest group in the pattern, reverse the order within the groups and descend: 8–5–3, 5–3–1, etc. This exercise sounds a bit like a bugle fanfare.

Play all the way up and down on each pattern. Apply to minor arpeggios, too.

Track 23

C Major Triad Arpeggio, Groups of Three in Triplets, Pattern 3

Ascending Descending

### Reverse Groups of Three

Play each group from the previous exercise backwards: 5–3–1, 8–5–3, 10–8–5, etc. When you reach the top note in the pattern and start back down, play ascending groups: 3–5–8, 1–3–5, etc. Apply to minor triad arpeggios as well.

Track 24

C Major Triad Arpeggio, Reversed Groups of 3 in Triplets, Pattern 3

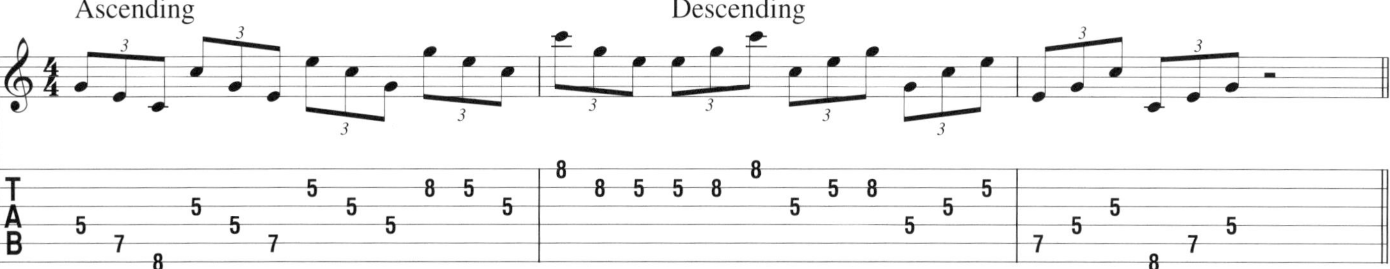

### Groups of Two: The Cadenza Exercise

This one reminds me of the cadenzas in classical violin concertos. Try it as a lick when you want to play a lot of notes but stay within one chord. Play descending 3rds, climbing up an arpeggio: 3–1, 5–3, 8–5, and so on, until you turn around and come back down with the pattern in reverse: 5–8, 3–5, 1–3, etc. Practice in the other patterns and with minor triad arpeggios as well.

Track 25

C Major Triad Arpeggio, Groups of Two, Pattern 3

Ascending Descending

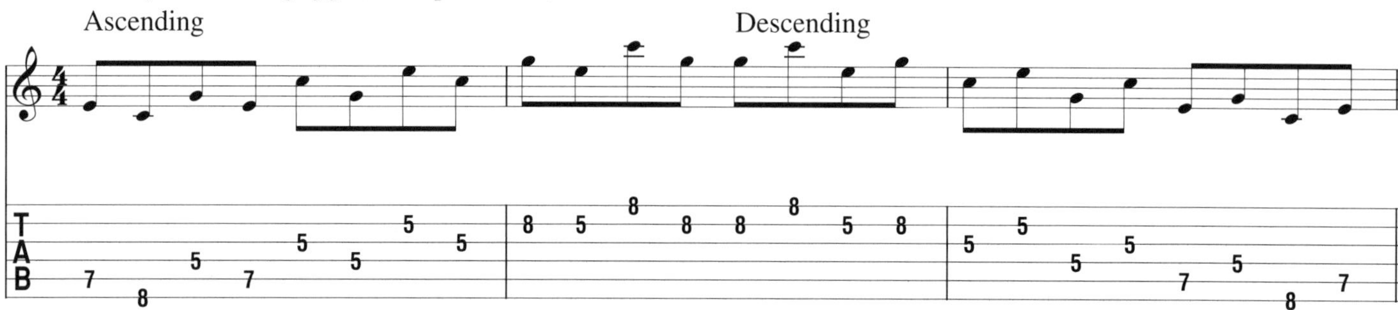


## Cool Triad Arpeggio Licks

Here's some ear candy to reward you for learning your triad arpeggios.

Over a dominant seventh chord, play its major triad and another one a whole step below for an easy-to-play but musical phrase.

Track 26

On minor 7th chords, alternate a minor triad with a major triad a whole step down.

Track 27

Ami7

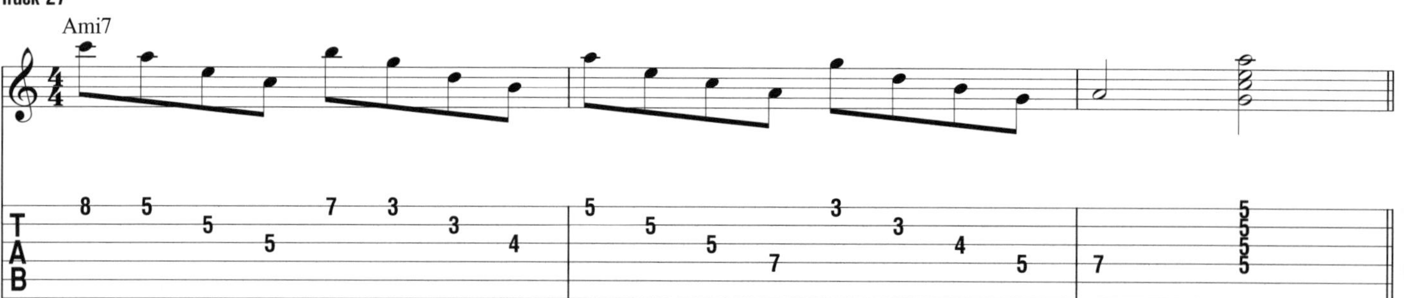

Track 28

Add a 6th to a raked minor triad for Jimi Hendrix's famous "Red House" blues lick.

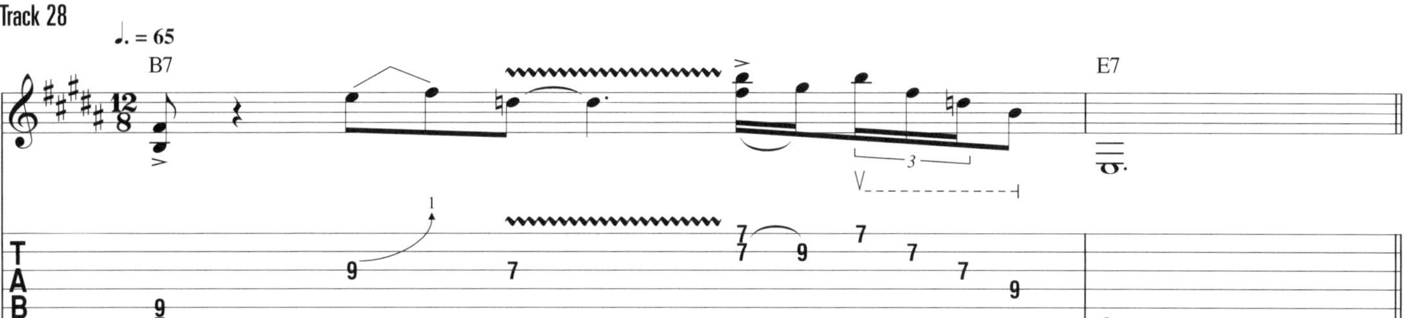


## Scale Review: Groups of Four in Triplets

For an interesting variation, play the group-of-four exercise from Chapter 6 in triplets instead of eighth notes. The best way to get it going is to memorize the first six notes (two beats) by rote. Just consider it as a short melody you are learning. Don't think too much about the actual four-note groups of notes. Work that first chunk up to a medium tempo. When it's under your fingers, slow down and add another six-note chunk, moving up through the other groups.

Track 29

C Major Scale, Groups of Four in Triplets, Pattern 2
Divided into Chunks

Chunks Joined
Ascending

Descending

# Seventh Chords and Arpeggios

By adding a 7th to a triad, we get a four-note seventh chord or arpeggio.

## Major Seventh

This is a major triad with a major 7th added to it. The notes are 1–3–5–7.

### Dma7 Arpeggios and Stock Chord Voicings

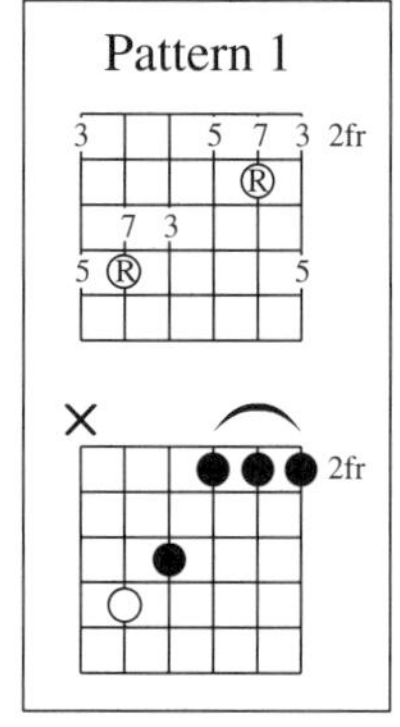

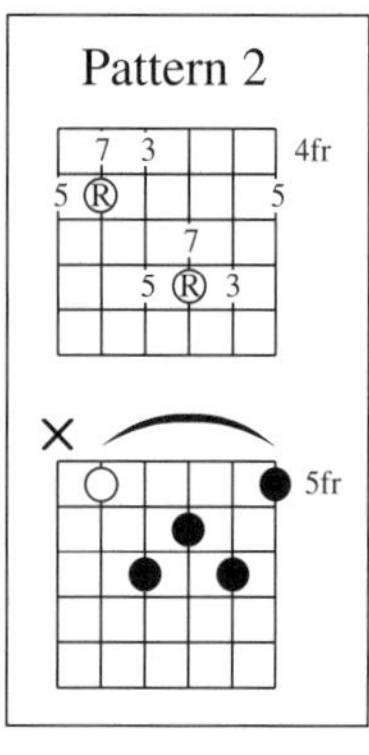

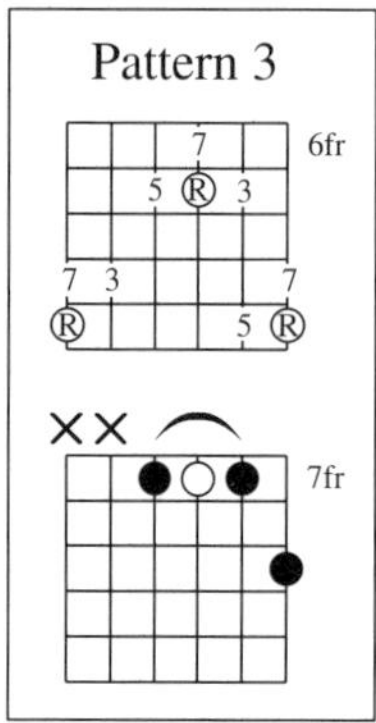

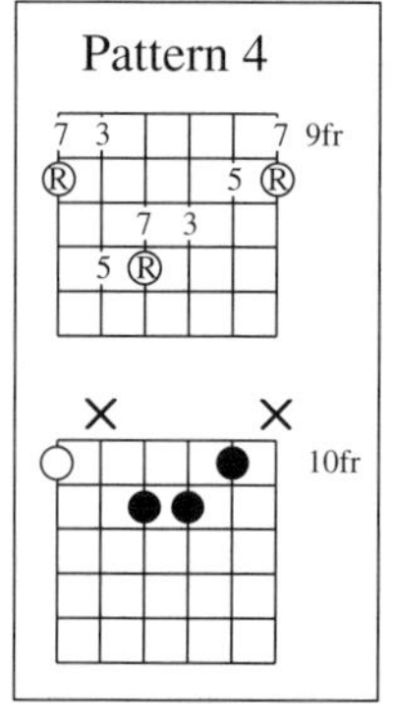

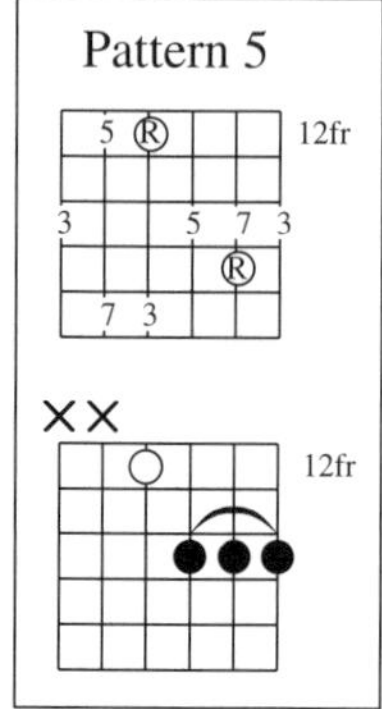


## Dominant Seventh

When a major triad has a minor seventh added to it, the result is called a dominant seventh chord. The notes of a dominant seventh chord or arpeggio are 1–3–5–♭7. The dominant chord quality is implied by simply adding a "7" or higher odd number to the chord name: D7, D9, D11, D13.

### D7 Arpeggios and Stock Chord Voicings

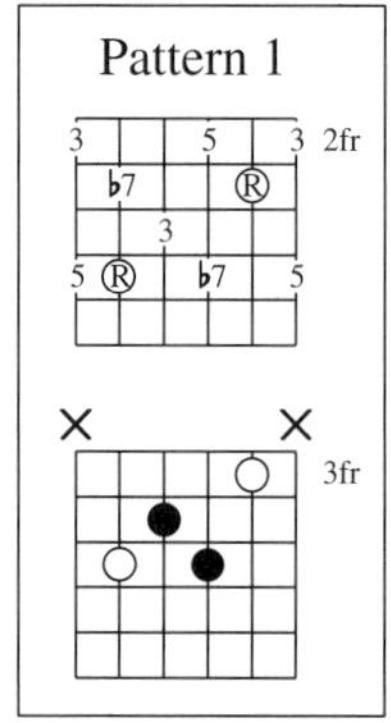

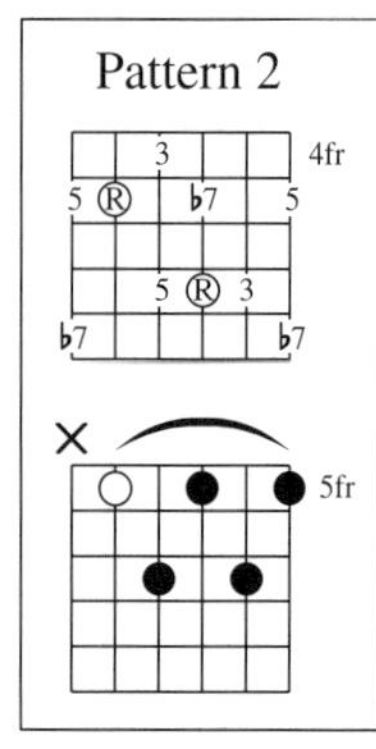

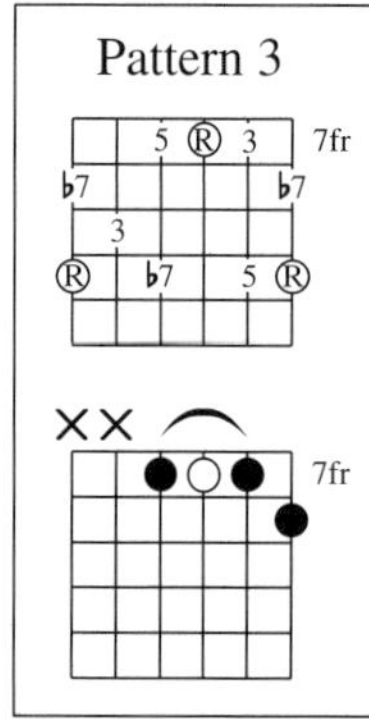

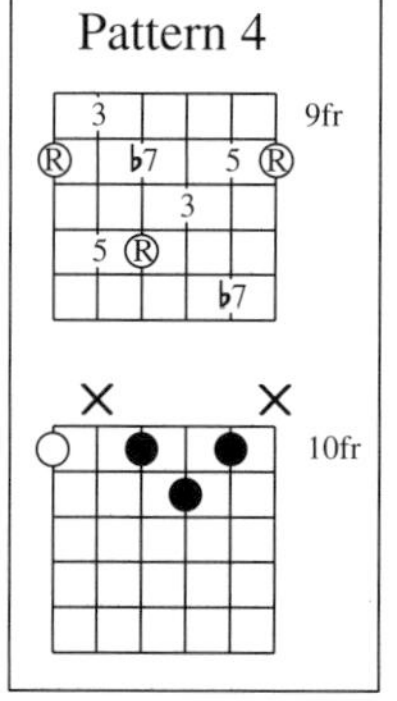

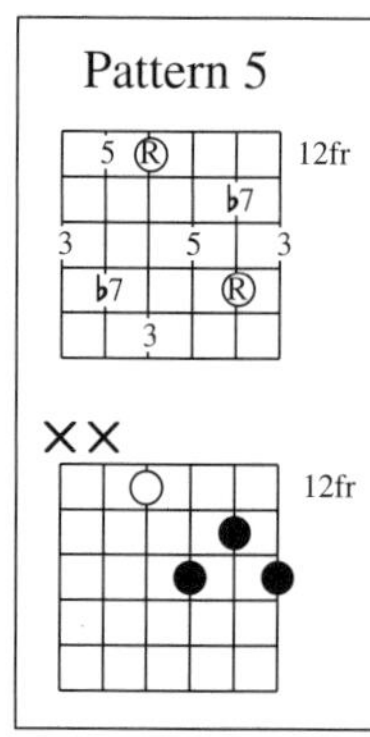


## Minor Seventh

When a minor triad has a minor seventh added, it's called a minor seventh arpeggio. The notes are 1–♭3–5–♭7.

### Dmi7 Arpeggios and Stock Chord Voicings

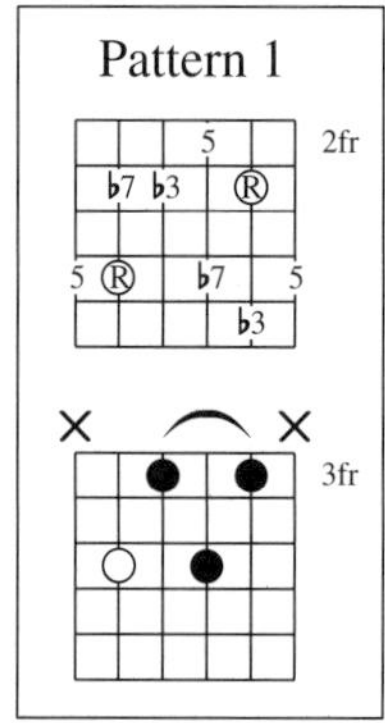

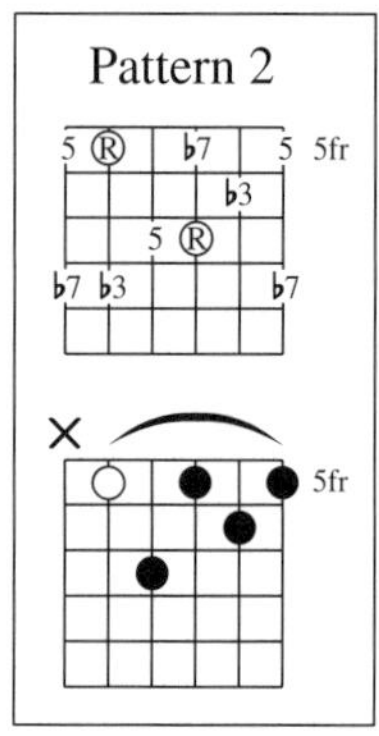

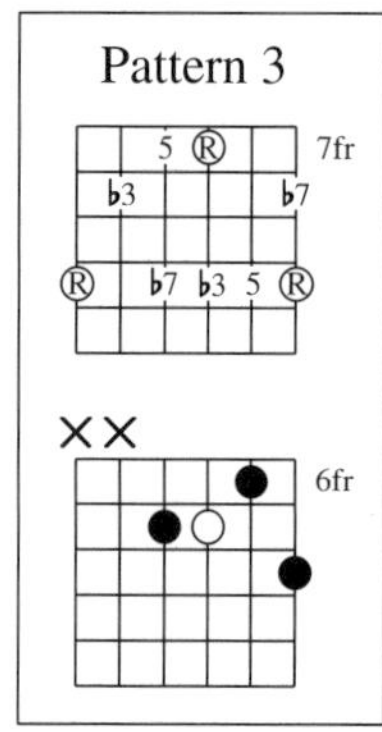

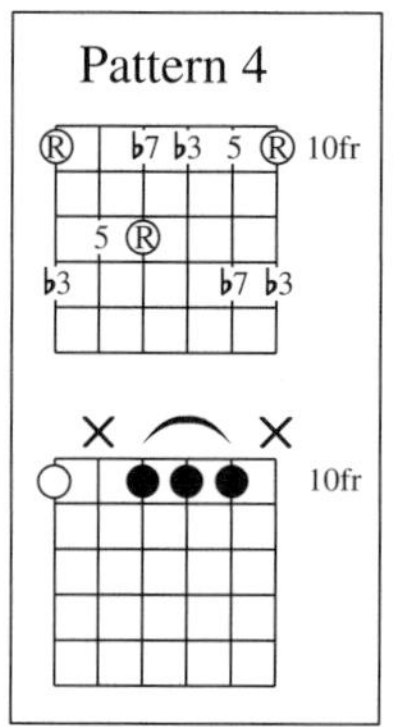

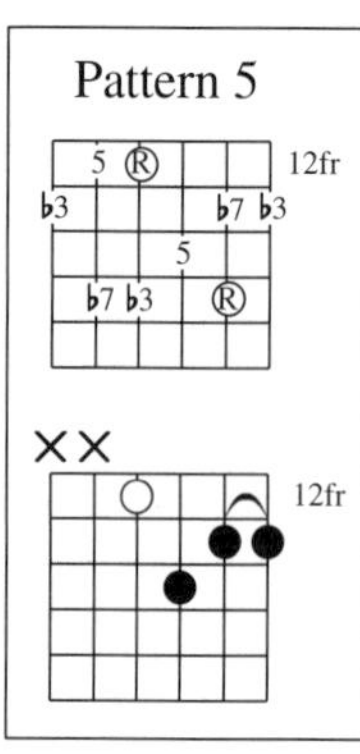

### Minor Seventh Flat Five

When a diminished triad has a minor 7th added to it, the result is a mi7(♭5) chord. Another popular name for this chord is *half-diminished* seventh (or simply half-diminished). The notes are 1–♭3–♭5–♭7.

**Dmi7(♭5) Arpeggios and Stock Chord Voicings**

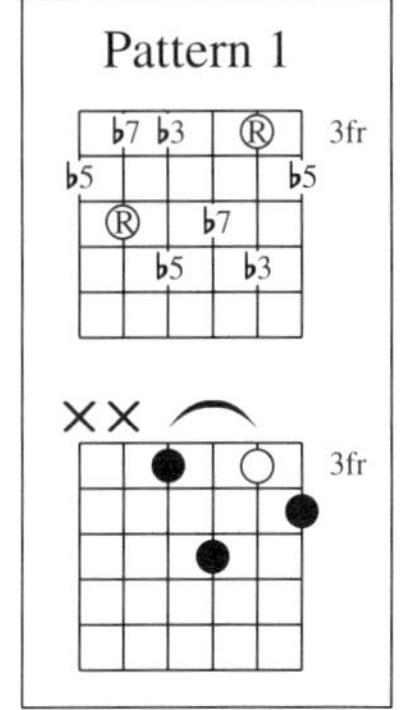


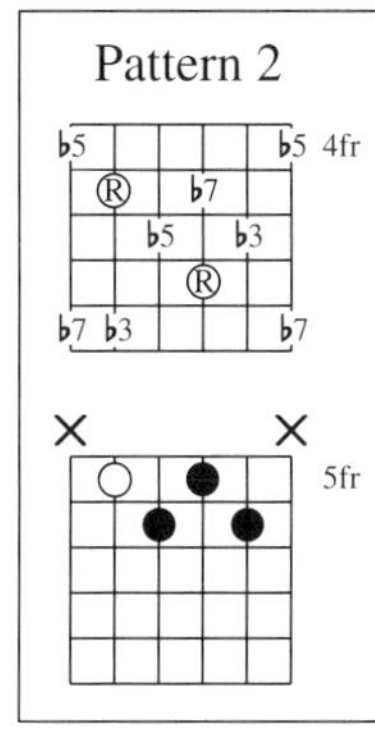


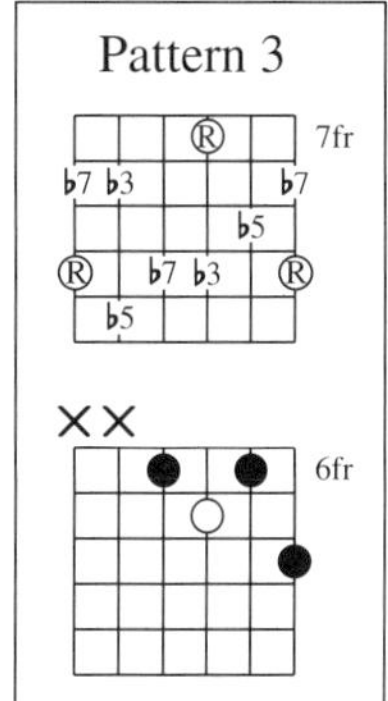


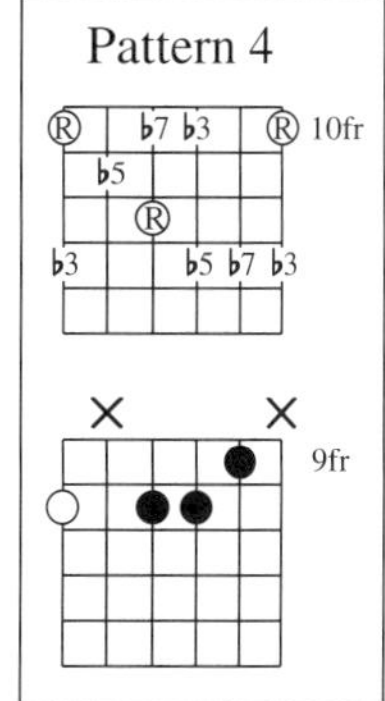


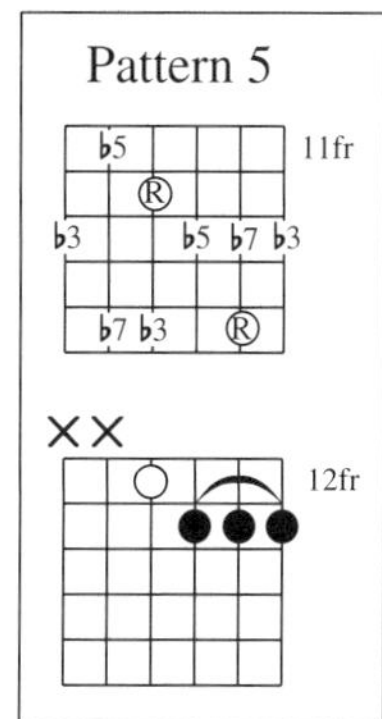


### Diminished Seventh

The diminished seventh chord is produced by adding a diminished 7th to a diminished triad. As contrasted to the mi7(♭5) (*half*-diminished seventh) chord, this one is *fully* diminished. There is always a minor 3rd interval between any two neighboring notes: 1–♭3–♭5–♭♭7, resulting in a parallel structure and repeating fretboard shapes. In these diagrams, each shape may be considered a D, F, A♭, or B diminished 7th chord or arpeggio. Any of its notes may be considered a root (or any other chord tone).

**D°7, F°7, A♭°7, B°7 Arpeggios and Stock Chord Voicings**

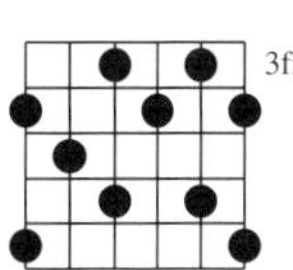


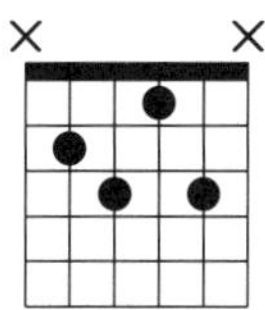

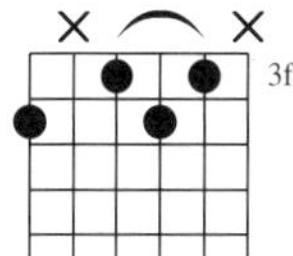


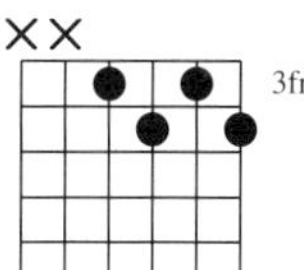


### Minor/Major Seventh

As the name states, this is a minor triad with a major seventh added: 1–♭3–5–7

**Dmi(ma7) Arpeggios and Stock Chord Voicings**

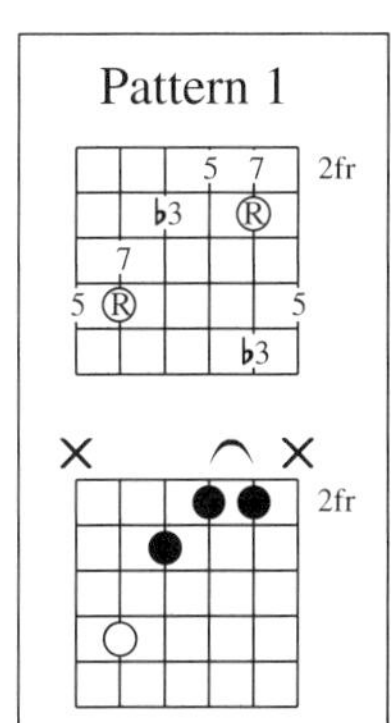


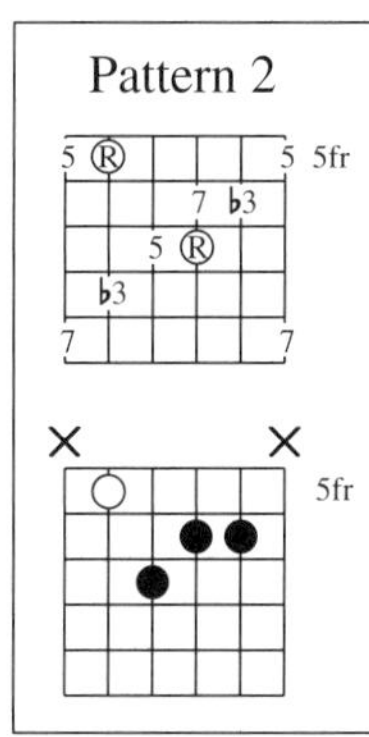


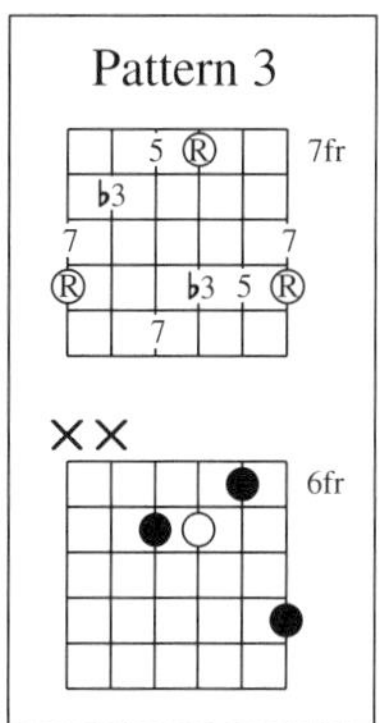


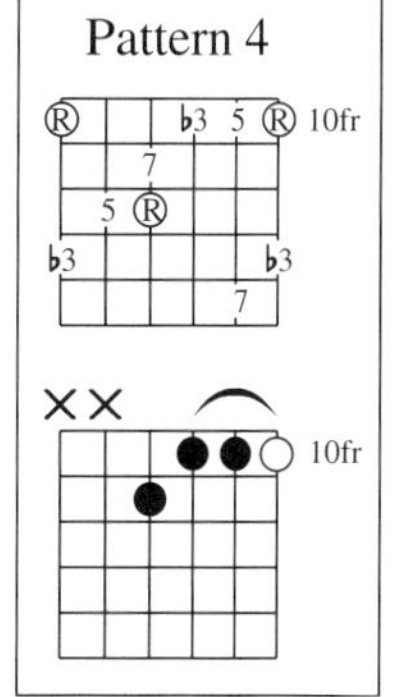


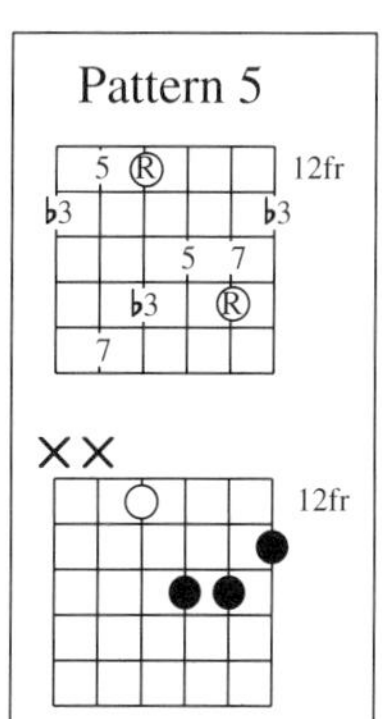

## Inversions and Slash Notation

We briefly touched on the *inversion* concept in the discussion of intervals. The term is also used to describe the arrangement of notes (*voicing*) of a chord.

- When its root is the lowest note played, a chord is said to be in *root position.* Root-position chords are not inverted, because the root is in the bass.

In a *slash chord,* a triad or seventh chord is superimposed over a bass note that is not the root of the chord. The way to read these aloud is "this over that"—e.g., "A over B." When the bass note is a chord tone, the slash chord is a way of specifying an inversion. Here are a few examples of the many possible inverted chord voicings.

- When its 3rd is the lowest note played, the chord is in *first inversion.*

- When its 5th is the lowest note played, the chord is in *second inversion.*

- When its 7th is the lowest note played, the chord is in *third inversion.* Since the 7th is on the right side of the slash, we can leave it out of the name to the left of the slash. Thus a third-inversion Gma7 chord is called G/F♯; a third-inversion Gmi7 chord is called Gmi/F, etc.

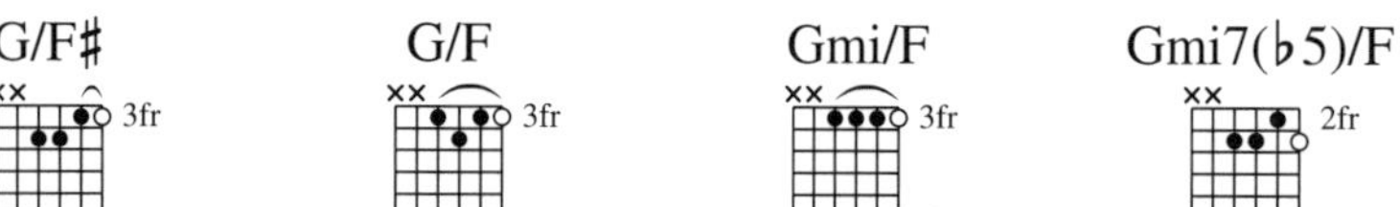


Mi/ma7 chords often appear in third inversion, when a descending bass line is played beneath a minor triad.

We don't have to think about diminished chords as inversions because the notes are all an equal distance apart, making any note in the chord a possible root, ♭3rd, ♭5th, or ♭♭7th. For example, when you want a C°7 chord in first inversion, just write E♭°7 instead. The two chords are equal.

When the note to the right of the slash is not a member of the chord to the left, we have a true *slash chord* (also known as an *upper structure*): a shorthand way of spelling a complicated (extended or altered) chord to make it easier to read and play.

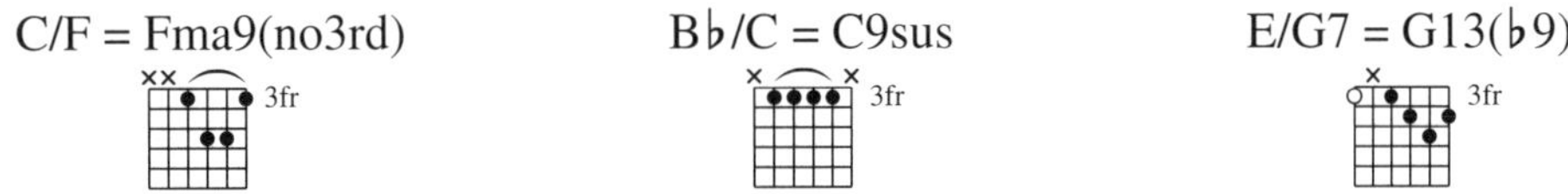


Though we need to understand and play these inversions and slash chords in rhythm parts, we can arpeggiate chords without following the written inversion when soloing. In other words, any of the tones in the chord (to the left of the slash) or the bass note (to the right) may be used as a target.

## Burn 'Em In

Add the various seventh chords and arpeggios in all twelve keys to your controlled practice schedule. Take as long as you need (two weeks is a good start) for each pattern of arpeggio shapes, starting with pattern 4 of each type. Make diagrams of them, recite the fretboard locations of the notes, and play them until you can produce them from memory. When you have one memorized, start the metronome and practice the new arpeggio in groups of three, groups of four, and the "cadenza exercise", as we did with the triad arpeggios.

# 9 Diatonic Harmony

In any major key there are seven basic chords, known as the diatonic chords. These chords are created by using every other note of the major scale. There is one chord for each unique note of the scale.

We already use Arabic numerals to describe scale degrees, intervals, strings, frets, fingers, and patterns. To help clarify things, Roman numerals are used to name the chords in a key. We use capital Roman numerals for major chords, and lowercase for minor and diminished chords. In our initial study of analyzing key centers, we'll use four-note seventh chords. Triads are more ambiguous and can fit into more different keys, so we'll deal with them next.

The easiest starting point is with the C major scale, but this exercise should be written out (by you) in all twelve keys, in English letters and Roman numerals, on staff paper. It's a bit of work, but knowing how to quickly find (if not memorize) diatonic chords is an essential skill. Write your scales out using whole notes (you know, those tiny footballs). Start low on the staff or below it, spreading each scale out evenly over half a staff. Continue past one octave so that thirteen scale notes are written; you can take up the full line.

The I ("one") chord uses the 1st, 3rd, 5th, and 7th notes of the scale. In the key of C, those notes are C–E–G–B. Connect these notes (in the lower octave of the scale only) on your staff paper. Now you can still plainly see the C major scale on the staff, and also which notes from the scale comprise the first chord, Cma7.

The interval between C and E is two whole steps, making it a major 3rd. From C to G is a perfect 5th, and from C to B is a major 7th. Now, draw in the 3rd, 5th, and 7th over middle C, making a stack of four footballs, one per line: C–E–G–B. Write out the names of the notes below the staff and the name of the chord above the staff.

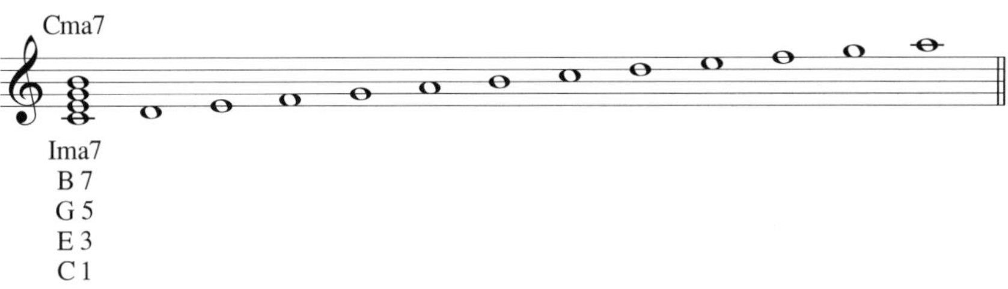

The ii chord uses the 2nd, 4th, 6th, and 8th notes of the scale. Internally, the notes in relation to D are 1–♭3–5–♭7. Check for yourself that from D to F is a minor 3rd: a whole step from D to E, plus a half step from E to F makes for a minor 3rd interval. Check them all out and notice that the intervals contained in the chord fit the name, Dmi7. Connect the notes D–F–A–C, showing how the ii chord is derived also from the C major scale, though the ii chord is actually minor.

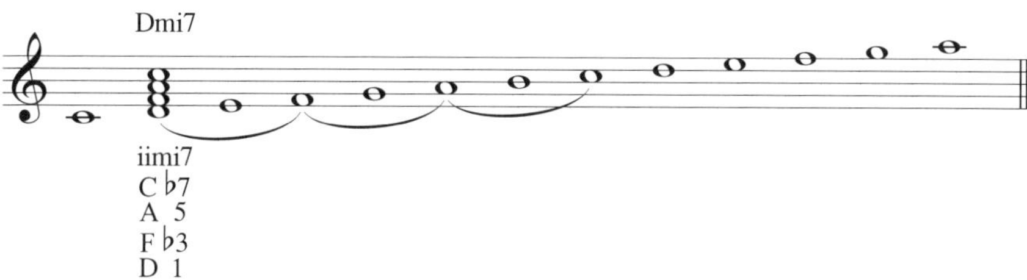


This is our first encounter with the notion that we can think of notes as being part of two things at once, a powerful idea that musicians use. Here we've seen that the chord found on step ii contains degrees 2–4–6–8 of the major scale. On its own, however, it's a minor seventh chord, spelled 1–♭3–5–♭7 from its root. We need to know what the notes are in relation to the root (in this case, D) of the current chord *and* in relation to the key center (in this case, C).

Repeat the process with the iii, IV, V, vi, and vii chords. (You'll see why I had you write thirteen notes of the scale.) Look at each note in every chord and count out what interval it is from the root.

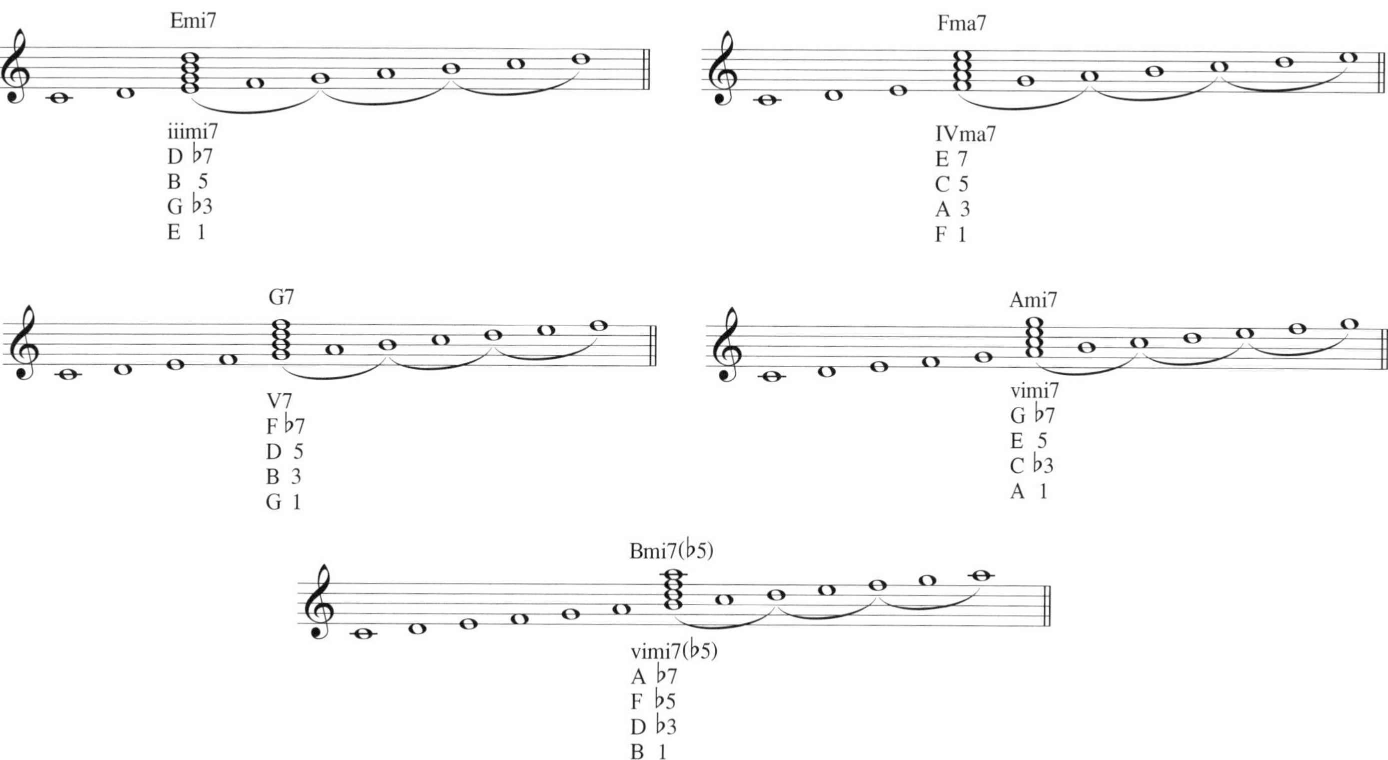

The I and IV chords are of the major-seventh quality. The ii, iii, and vi are minor-seventh chords. There are two chords of singular nature: V and vii, both containing an internal tritone (♭5) interval. The V is a dominant seventh chord, with a major 3rd but a minor 7th. The vii is the mi7(♭5) or half-diminished: 1–♭3–♭5–♭7.

> The name of a chord is usually based on at least one of the intervals it contains, with the other intervals being implied. In the ma7 chord, the suffix "ma7" by itself implies the complete spelling 1–3–5–7. The "mi7" suffix implies a minor seventh chord, spelled 1–♭3–5–♭7. An exception is the dominant chord (1–3–5–♭7), which has only a number after the chord letter; it gets its name from the scale degree it is usually based on (V).

Write out the different keys, one for each line of your staff paper, each one a 4th higher (or 5th lower) than the last: C–F–B♭–E♭–A♭–D♭–G♭–B–E–A–D–G. Put each sharp or flat where it needs to be for every note. (Do not use key signatures at the beginning of the line.) Write out the diatonic chords in all twelve keys. If you remember the major scale formula (see Chapter 6), you can spell out the scales in all twelve keys, giving you all the notes of the diatonic chords in each major key. To show you how it will look, here are the diatonic chords in the key of F major.

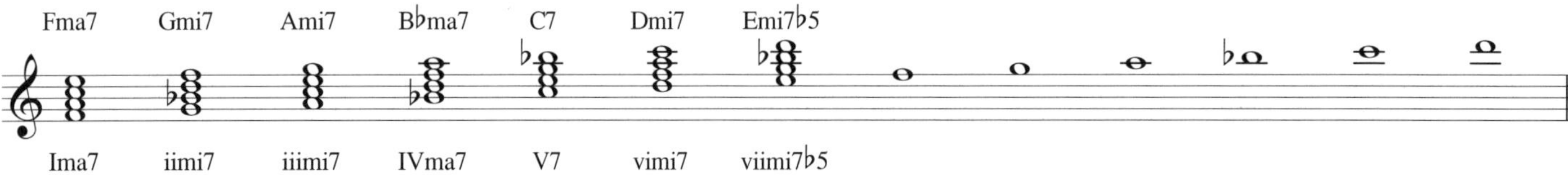


When you start going crazy from this, consider what you can learn from it:

1. The order of chord qualities in any major key: ma7–mi7–mi7–ma7–dom7–mi7–mi7(♭5); memorize this just as you memorize the major scale formula.

2. The intervallic distance between notes of the chords: in a dominant chord, from 5 to 7 is a minor 3rd, etc.

3. The intervallic distance between the roots of the chords: from iii to V is a minor 3rd, from IV to vii is an augmented 4th, etc.

4. What the notes in these chords are in relation to the overall key center. For instance, the 5th of the vi chord is the 3rd of the scale. In A, that vi chord is F♯mi, and the note is C♯.

5. What the notes in the chords are in relation to the other chords in the same key. For instance, the 3rd of the I chord is the 7th of the IV chord. Knowing this, you can tell what'll happen if you keep playing a particular note while the chords change.

6. Eventually you will have the diatonic chords in commonly used keys completely memorized.

## Diatonic Seventh Chord and Arpeggio Exercises

Play the F major scale, harmonized in pattern-4 seventh chords with roots on the sixth string, up and down the fingerboard. If we stick with these chords only, we're staying in, or diatonic to, the key of F major.

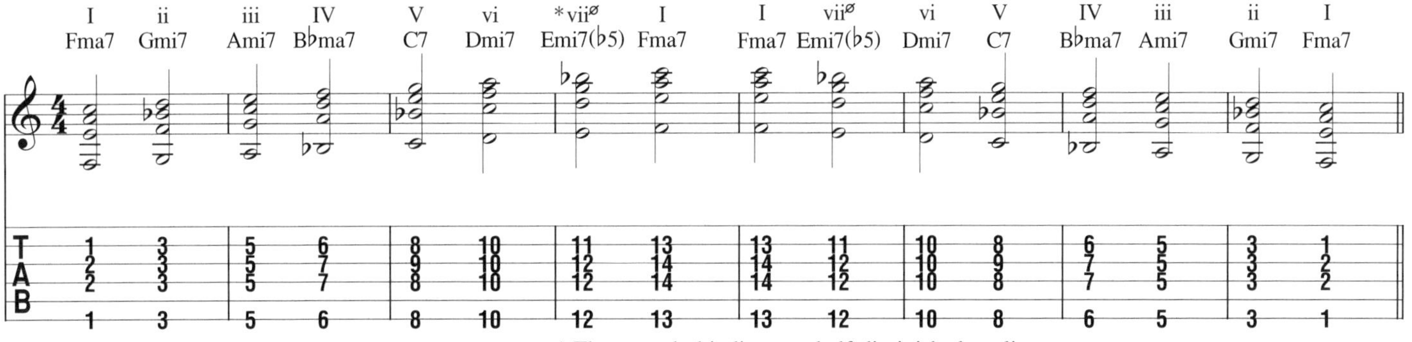


* The ø symbol indicates a half-diminished quality.

Play the B♭ major scale, harmonized in pattern-2 seventh chords with roots on the fifth string, up and down the fingerboard.

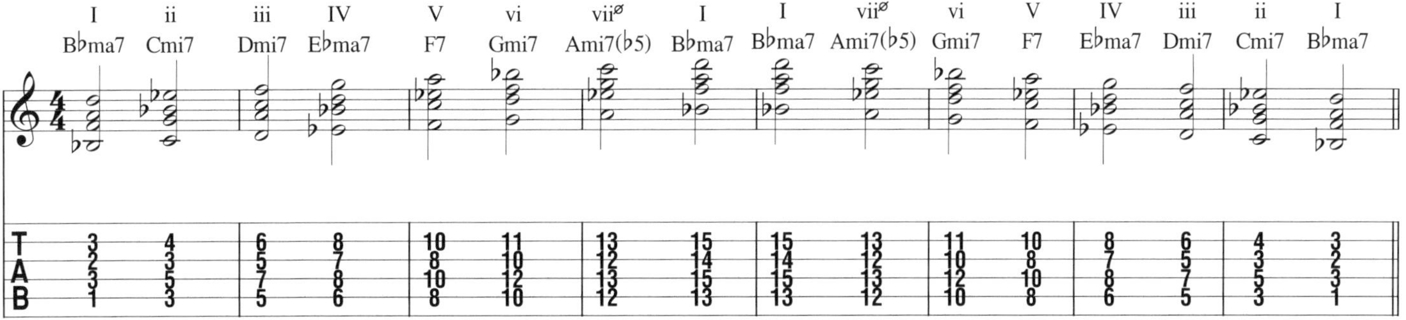


Play the E♭ major scale, harmonized in pattern-5 seventh chords with roots on the fourth string, up and down the fingerboard.

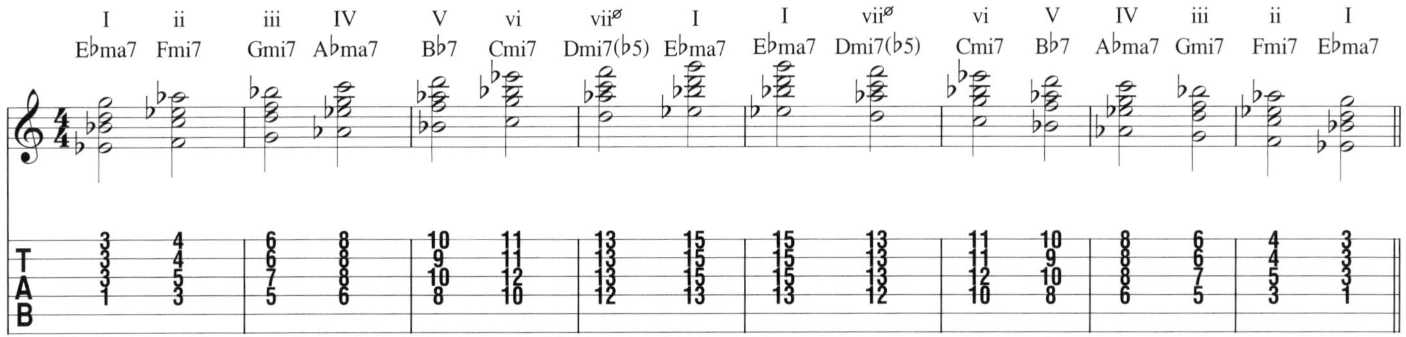

Play all the diatonic seventh arpeggios in one key in the same position. The sequence of notes for these is 1–3–5–7, 2–4–6–8, 3–5–7–9, etc. Be careful with the mi7(♭5) arpeggio on step vii. The sequence is shown here in C, pattern 4. Gradually work this exercise out for all five patterns. Also try mixing up the order and alternating ascending and descending arpeggios (1–3–5–7, 8–6–4–2, etc.).

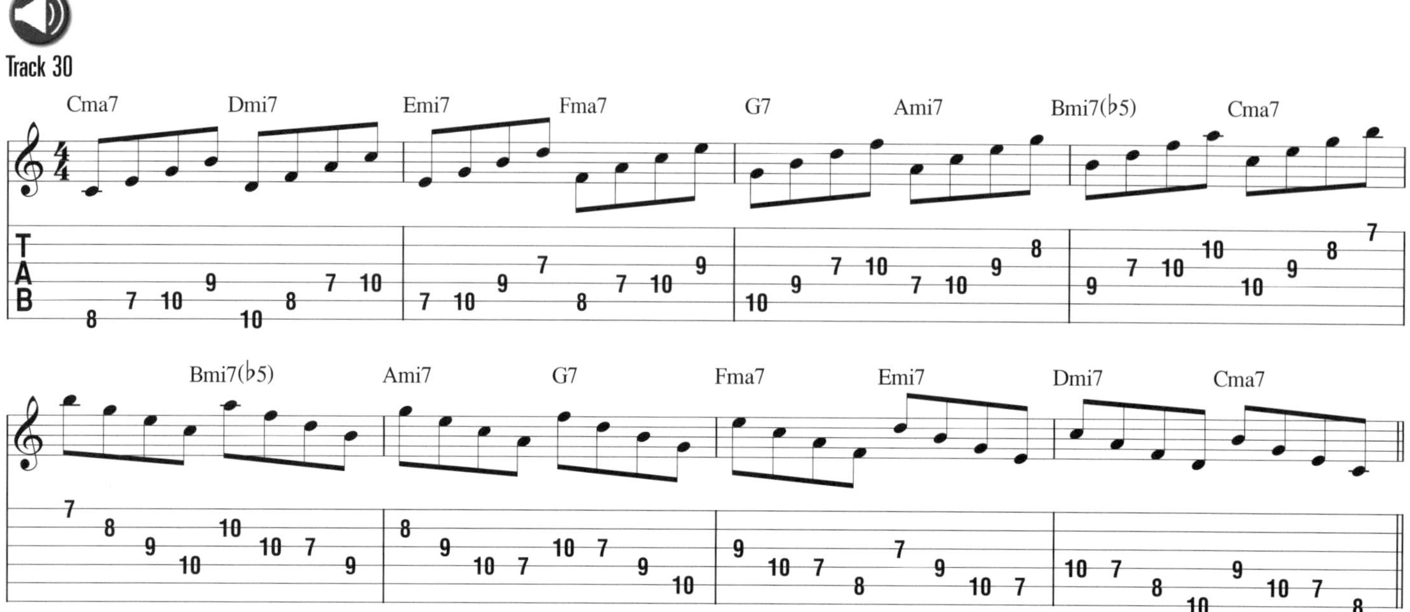


Outline I–ii–V–I progressions with seventh arpeggios in each major key through a cycle of 4ths, starting in the key of C, then F, then B♭, etc. Play only one measure on each chord. The arpeggios in the examples start on the roots, but when you become familiar with them, try starting the first arpeggio from any of its notes. Then when it's time to switch, move by the shortest possible distance to a note in the next arpeggio.

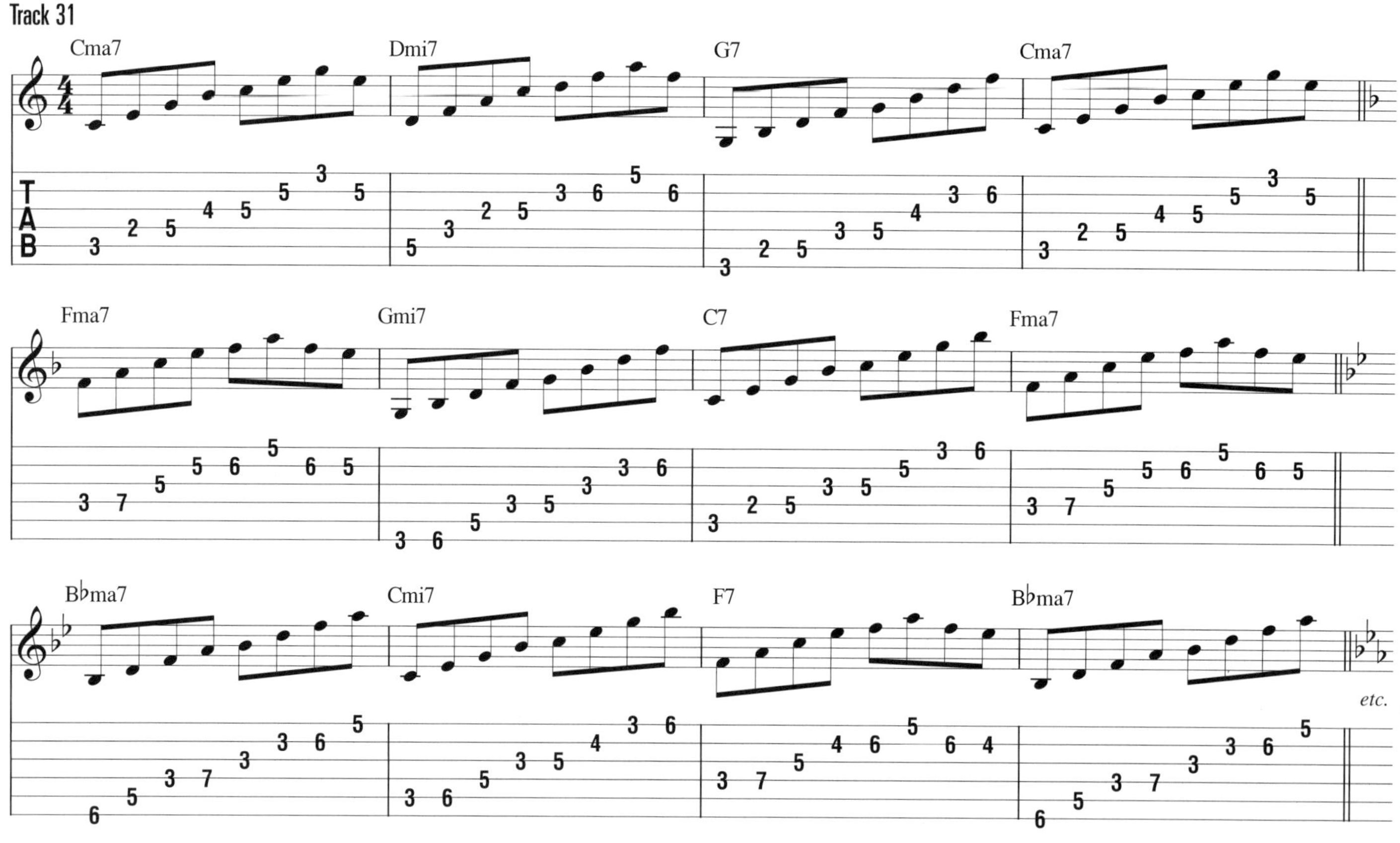

## Diatonic Harmony in Triads

By removing the 7th of each chord, we can see that everything we've just learned about diatonic harmony also holds true for triads. We have major triads on steps I, IV, and V, minor triads on ii, iii, and vi, and a diminished triad on vii. Memorize the order of triad qualities in a harmonized major scale.

| Ma | mi | mi | Ma | Ma | mi | dim |
|---|---|---|---|---|---|---|
| I | ii | iii | IV | V | vi | vii° |

## Diatonic Triad and Arpeggio Exercises

Play the F major scale, harmonized in pattern-4 triads with the roots on the fourth string, up and down the fingerboard. The E diminished triad found on vii° is spelled 1–♭3–♭5. These are all the diatonic triads in the key of F major.

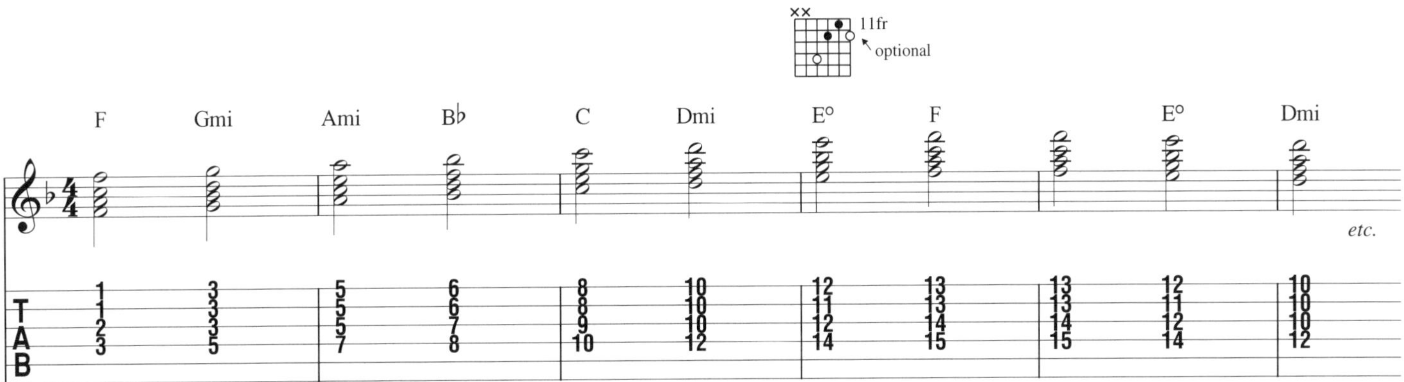


Now play the B♭ major scale, harmonized in pattern-2 triads with the roots on the fifth string, up and down the fingerboard. These are all the triads in the key of B♭ major.

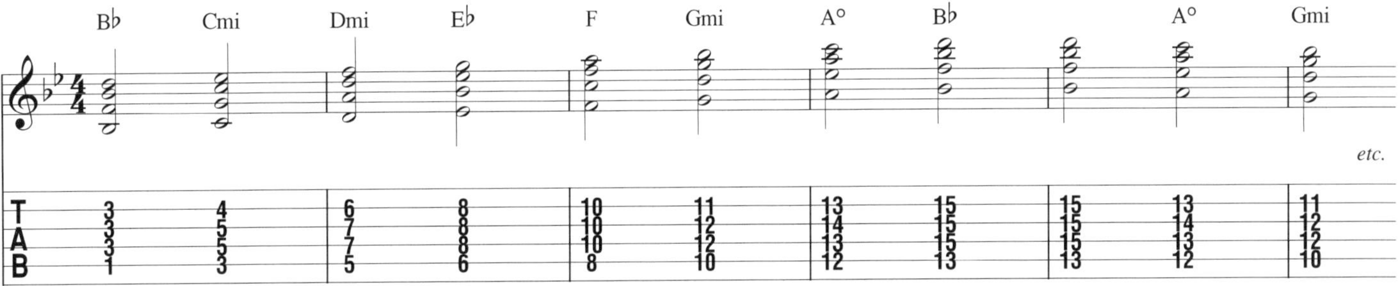

Next we'll play all the diatonic triads in one key as arpeggios in the same position. Because there are three notes in a triad, we'll play this example in 3/4 time; just count to three instead of four. As an interval study, the sequence of notes is 1–3–5, 2–4–6, 3–5–7, etc. Watch out for the diminished arpeggio on step 7.

Track 32

Triads in C Major, Pattern 4

Returning to eighth notes in 4/4 time, play I–IV–V–I progressions with major triad arpeggios in each major key through a cycle of 4ths. Again, start by playing these from the roots, but eventually you'll want to connect them more smoothly.

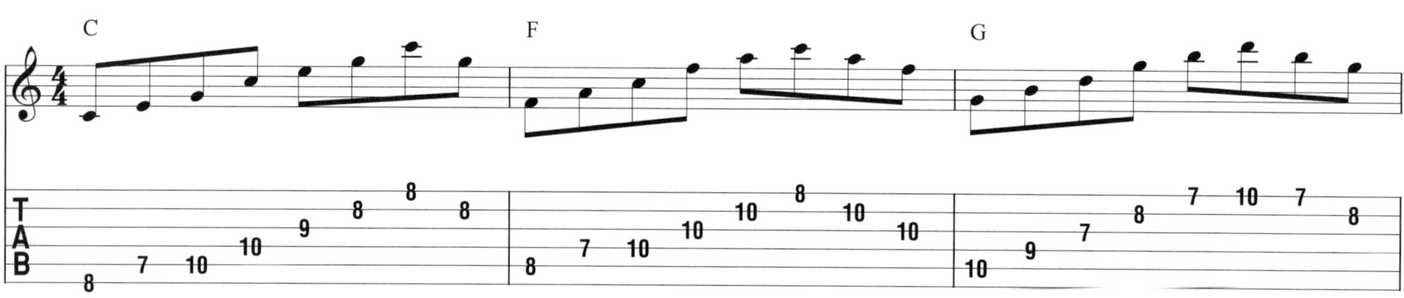


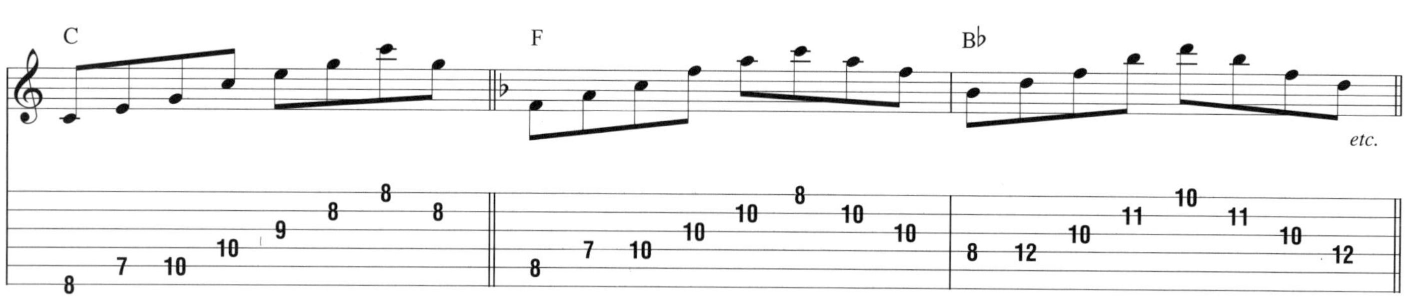

# 10 Finding Key Centers

Key centers allow us to fit one scale over an entire chord progression, though without specifying which notes of the scale are to be hit on a particular chord. Learn to play with the general key-center approach before refining it with the more specific chord-tone approach.

We'll perform a *harmonic analysis* of a diatonic chord progression, based on the major-scale harmony we just learned. Suppose we have the following three chords:

E♭ma7 Dmi7 F7

Because it is a major seventh chord, you'll remember, E♭ma7 may be I, or it may be IV. Therefore, this chord is diatonic to either the key of E♭ major or B♭ major.

| I | ii | iii | IV | V | vi | viiø |
|---|---|---|---|---|---|---|
| E♭ma7 | Fmi7 | Gmi7 | A♭ma7 | B♭7 | Cmi7 | Dmi7(♭5) |

| I | ii | iii | IV | V | vi | viiø |
|---|---|---|---|---|---|---|
| B♭ma7 | Cmi7 | Dmi7 | E♭ma7 | F7 | Gmi7 | Ami7(♭5) |

Look at the second chord of the progression, Dmi7. Because it's a minor seventh chord, it may be ii, iii, or vi. Therefore, its possible keys are C, B♭, or F. At this point, we can say positively that the first two chords are only common to the key of B♭.

Looking at F7, and, of course, all chords must be analyzed because we never know when the key might change, we realize that the diatonic harmony we know only includes a dominant chord in one place: the V. Counting down the major scale formula from V to I, we see that F7 is the V in the key of B♭.

Therefore, the B♭ major scale may be played over the entire progression.

The harmonic analysis looks like this:

| E♭ma7 | Dmi7 | F7 |
|---|---|---|
| B♭: IV | iii | V |

Analyze these short progressions, providing possible Roman numerals for each, and tell which major key(s) they might be in. If there are two possible keys, put the second analysis on a new line. Note: Whenever there is dominant seventh chord or mi7(♭5) chord, only one major key is possible. Don't worry about minor keys right now.

1. Fma7–Dmi7–C7

2. C♯mi7–F♯mi7

3. Ami7–Cma7–Emi7

4. B♭mi7–Fmi7–A♭7

5. Fma7–Cma7

6. F♯mi7(♭5)

## Finding Key Centers in Triad Progressions

Suppose we have a song or section that uses the triads B♭, C, and F.

B♭ C F

Remember that a chord with no specified quality is always a major triad. If a triad is major, we can try it as I, IV, or V. Here, we'll start with B♭; make it I, then see if the other chords will fit that key. The ii chord in B♭ is Cm, and we have C major here, so the key of B♭ won't work for us.

When we try out B♭ as the IV chord instead of as the I, we can see that two major chords a whole step apart coincide with IV and V in major harmony. We can put B♭ and C on IV and V, respectively, and count down or up using the major scale formula to find I. If the F chord fits into the formula, it is also part of the key center. This progression turns out to be a IV–V–I in F major, so we can play the F major scale over all of it.

| F | Gmi | Ami | B♭ | C | Dmi | E° | F |
|---|---|---|---|---|---|---|---|
| I | ii | iii | IV | V | vi | vii° | I |

Let's do this again to review. Another common progression is F♯mi–B–E–A (it's used at the end of the verses in "Layla"). First we have a minor chord, which may be ii, iii, or vi. We can try each possibility and see which key center best fits the other chords.

If F♯mi is ii, then we count down one whole step to find I (E). Following the order of chord qualities and major scale formula, we spell the chords in the key of E major.

| E | F♯mi | G♯mi | A | B | C♯mi | D♯° | E |
|---|---|---|---|---|---|---|---|
| I | ii | iii | IV | V | vi | vii° | I |

We got lucky and found the key center on the first try. All the chords of our "Layla" excerpt fit the key of E, so the E major scale applies. The progression is ii–V–I–IV.

What if we started out by trying F♯ minor as vi? We could count up from vi to VIII (or I): F♯–G♯–A, finding the key of A major.

| A | Bmi | C♯mi | D | E | F♯mi | G♯° | A |
|---|---|---|---|---|---|---|---|
| I | ii | iii | IV | V | vi | vii° | I |

However, our progression contains B major, and not Bmi, so we are not in A. Likewise, if we try treating F♯mi as the iii chord, we get the key of D major, which contains Emi and Bmi—even less of a match for our progression.

**Key-Center Exercise**

Find the correct major key(s) for the following progressions. Sometimes the chords will fit into more than one key.

1. D–F♯mi–Emi–A

2. G–Emi–D

3. Fmi–B♭–E♭–Cmi

4. C♯mi–A–E

5. B♭–E♭–Gmi–A°

6. A♭mi–B♭mi–C♭

# 11 Minor Scales and Keys

The *natural minor* scale is spelled 1 2 ^ ♭3 4 5 ^ ♭6 ♭7 8. This is the diatonic scale for most minor-key progressions. It differs from the major scale on steps 3, 6, and 7; these intervals are all minor in the minor scale. Here is a direct comparison; the half steps in both scales are marked with carets (^).

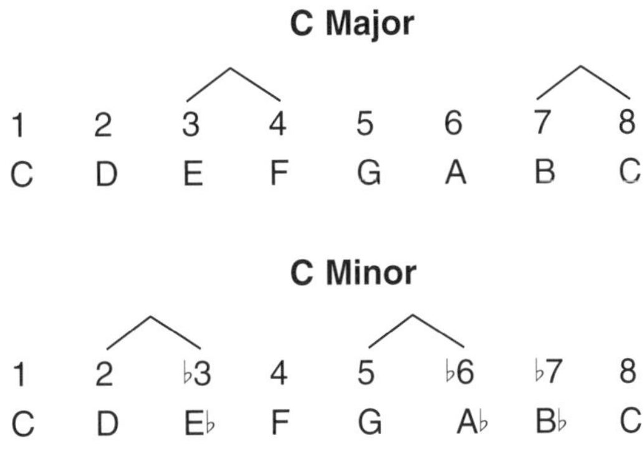


Memorize the fact that in the natural minor scale formula there are half steps from scale degrees 2 to 3 and from 5 to 6. So the minor scale formula looks like this:

Whole—half—Whole—Whole—half—Whole—Whole

## Relatives

If you align step 1 of the minor scale with step 6 of the major scale, the pattern of whole and half steps is the same. Below you see the major scale with half steps from 3–4 and 7–8, and the minor scale with half steps from 2–3 and 5–6. Notice the half steps are in the same places. The minor-scale formula is a displaced version of the major-scale formula.

| Major: | 1 | 2 | 3 | 4 | 5 | 6 | 7 | 1 | 2 | 3 | 4 | 5 | 6 |
|---|---|---|---|---|---|---|---|---|---|---|---|---|---|
| Minor: | | | | | | 1 | 2 | 3 | 4 | 5 | 6 | 7 | 8 |

This means if we start and end the major scale on step 6, we get a minor scale. In C major, the 6th is A, so we would get an A minor scale. The two scales overlap, using the same notes, with the major scale shown here on the top line, and the minor scale below.

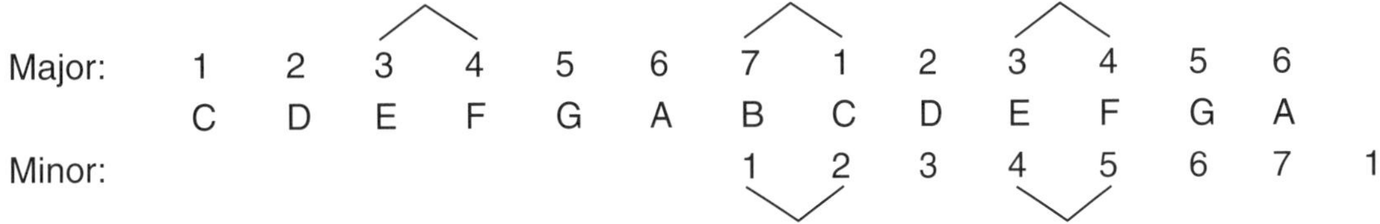

The two scales are *relatives* of each other. Each major scale has a relative minor, and each minor scale has a relative major. In the previous example, we see the C major scale along with its relative minor, A natural minor, created by treating the 6 as if it were 1. Since they share the same notes, relative major and minor keys have the same key signatures on the musical staff.

The principle of relatives is seen in the popular "three-fret" method for finding scales. The relative minor is always three frets below the root in any major-scale pattern. For instance, C major pattern 3 has a root on string 6, fret 8. We can find its relative, A minor, starting at string 6, fret 5. The pattern of notes does not change, but the numbers do. In the diagram below, the roots of the major scale are in circles, and the roots of the relative minor are in squares. In this example, C major pattern 3 = A minor pattern 4.

**C Major Pattern 3 = A Minor Pattern 4**

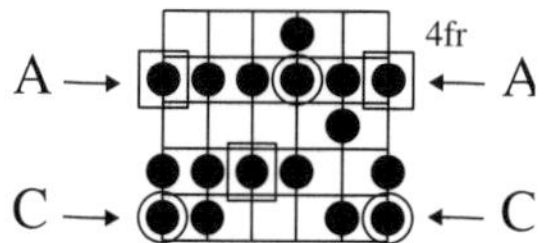


In a way, you already know all five patterns of minor scales if you learned major scale patterns 1–5. The catch is that even though the pattern of notes is exactly the same, the root shape and pattern number are different now, as are the numbers of all the scale degrees and, importantly, the chord tones. Your melodic phrasing will have to change according to the situation.

The same three-fret relationship applies in the opposite direction. If you already know a natural minor scale, you can stay in place (don't move!) and start it from the ♭3rd (three frets *up* the neck) to get the relative major. But even though the pattern of notes is the same, licks that you usually play in a minor context won't make a lot of sense over a major chord without some adaptation. You may find yourself hitting the 6th too often. I'll demonstrate this as simply as possible, but the same principle applies to phrases with more notes in them.

Track 33

Adapt the formerly minor lick to finish up on the root (or any other tone) of the major chord (C, in this case), and you'll be dead-on.

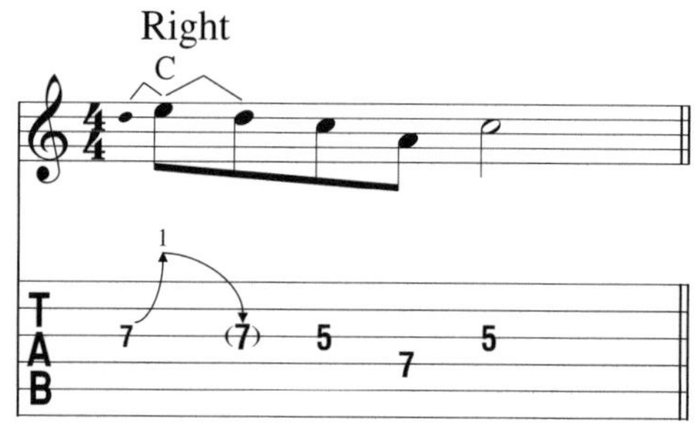

Here we see the two scales, surrounded by the rest of the root shapes: 1–5 in C, and from pattern 2 up to pattern 1 in A minor.

**C Major**

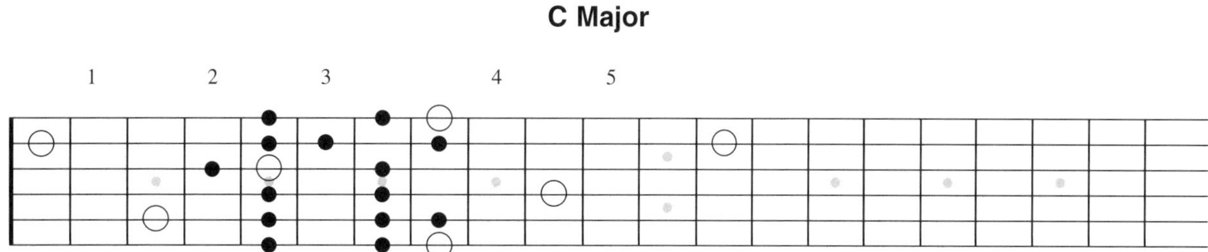


**A Minor**

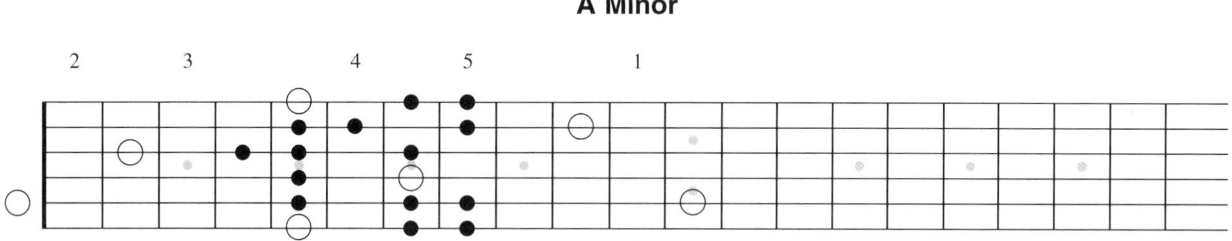


If you play all five patterns of major and relative minor, you'll notice each major pattern is the same as a minor pattern with a pattern number that is *one higher*. Play them all and see for yourself.

Pattern 1 Major = Pattern 2 Relative Minor
Pattern 2 Major = Pattern 3 Relative Minor
Pattern 3 Major = Pattern 4 Relative Minor
Pattern 4 Major = Pattern 5 Relative Minor
Pattern 5 Major = Pattern 1 Relative Minor

With practice, you'll be able to make this connection without thinking, slipping from one type of phrasing to another within the same fingering pattern to fit the most common key change: from a major key to its relative minor, or vice versa (from a minor key to its relative major).

### Sample Solos

Any examples on the CD that contain melodic structures or articulations (slides, bends, hammer-ons, etc.) are written out in case you want to study them and steal a few licks, and you're encouraged to do so. However, your priority should be improvising and composing your own solos.

## Playing Exercise

Check out the sample solo below, then dial it out and play over this chord progression using only one fingering pattern of the B♭ major scale. (Minimize any movement up and down the neck.) Emphasize the root of each chord when it occurs. Only when you're comfortable finding the roots on time should you move to another pattern that you know and start again, finding the roots (or other chord tones) there.

## Diatonic Minor Progressions

We've seen how the natural minor scale is structurally related to the major scale. It shares chords in the same way. The minor scale harmony is the same as its relative major's harmony, but starting on the vi chord. Thus, the chords in A minor are the same as the chords in C major. Here is the A minor scale, harmonized in seventh chords.

| Ami7 | Bmi7(♭5) | Cma7 | Dmi7 | Emi7 | Fma7 | G7 | Ami7 |
|---|---|---|---|---|---|---|---|
| i | iimi7(♭5) | ♭III | iv | v | ♭VI | ♭VII | i |

Here's the harmonized A natural minor scale in seventh-chord voicings in pattern 2:

**Pattern 2 Voicings**

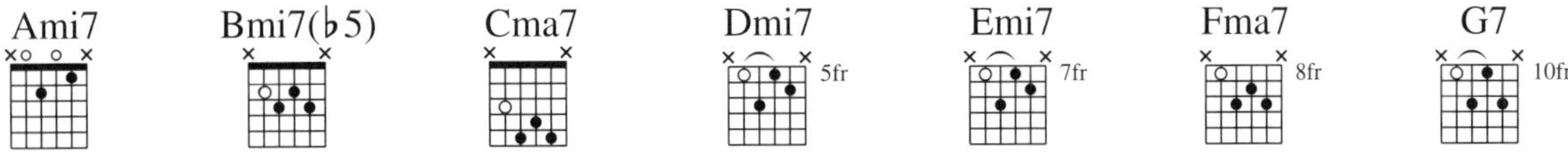


By removing the seventh from each chord, we get the triads, also using pattern 2. These are voiced on the top three strings only in this example.

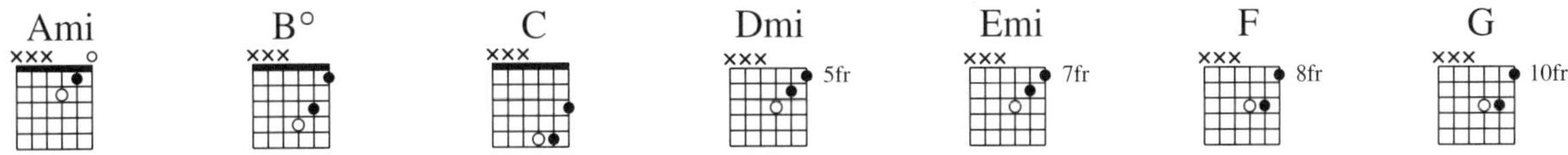


Listen to the sample solo, then dial it out and practice using the A natural minor scale over this progression.

Track 35

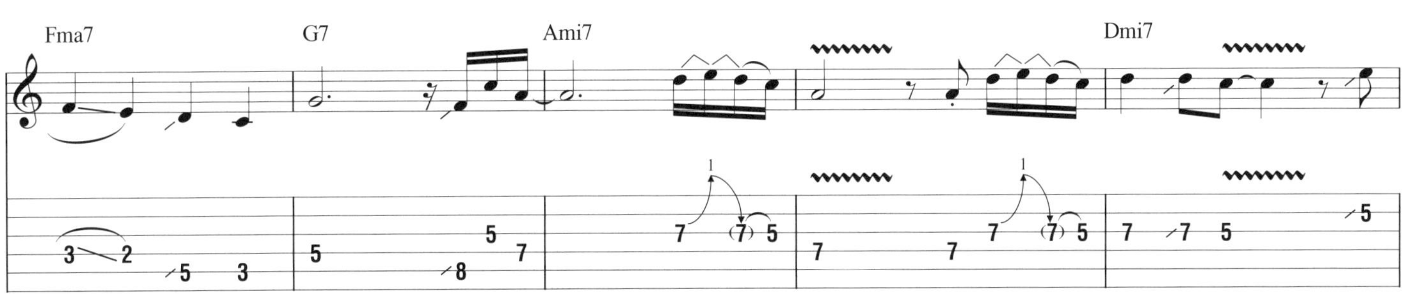


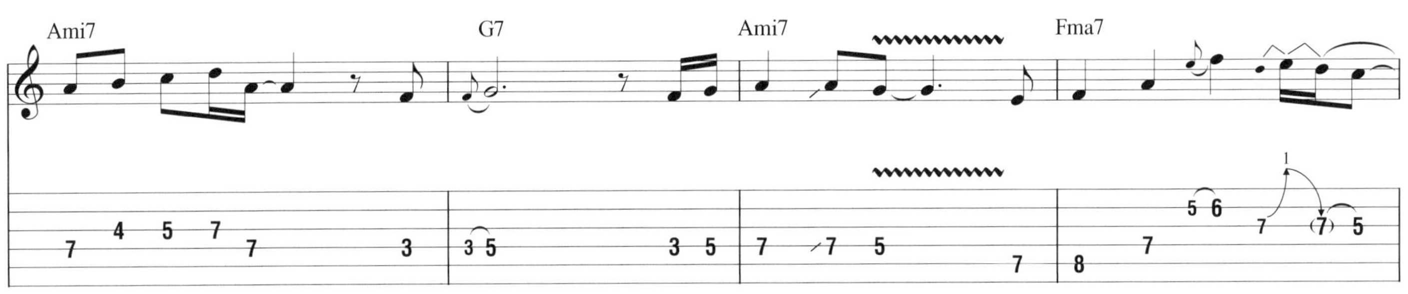

## 11

Cma7
G7
Ami7
Emi7
Dmi7
Fma7
G7
Ami7
Dmi7
Ami7
G7
Ami7
Fma7
Cma7
G7
Ami7

## Harmonic Minor

There is a common exception to know with regard to diatonic chords in minor keys. Often the v chord is changed from minor (Emi7 if the key is Ami) to dominant (E7). The note that changes when we do this is the 7th (G) of the overall key of A minor. It's raised to G♯. This raised 7th or *leading tone* creates a stronger pull toward A, the root of the i chord, which usually follows the V7. Of course we want to follow the change with our melodies and solos, too, so there is a scale that makes the same change: *harmonic minor*, spelled 1–2–♭3–4–5–♭6–7–8. It's identical to the natural minor scale, with the exception of the major 7th.

We must take this into account when analyzing minor progressions. Even though it is not strictly diatonic, the V chord can be changed from minor (vmi7) to dominant (V7). When using triads only, the v chord may be changed from minor (v) to major (V).

You can create fingerings for the harmonic minor scale by augmenting the ♭7th of the natural minor scale. Raising the 7th creates an augmented 2nd interval between steps 6 and 7 of this scale, which creates new fingering challenges. Whether you keep the 6th and 7th on the same strings or move to the next one will depend on which way is easiest at the time, so practice it both ways. Here is a pattern 1 and pattern 4 D harmonic minor scale with the two possibilities in parentheses.

**D Harmonic Minor**

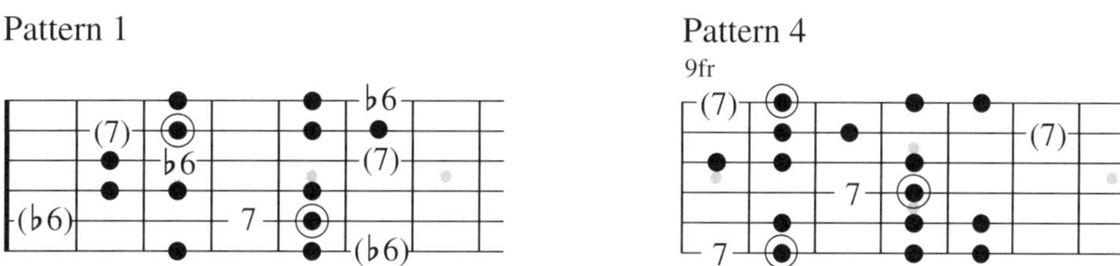


Listen to the sample solo, then dial it out and play the D *natural* minor scale over this progression. Switch to D *harmonic* minor over the V chord, using the raised 7th of the scale (C♯, the major 3rd of the V chord) as the target chord tone for that chord.

B♭ Dmi B♭ Dmi
B♭ A A/C♯ Dmi
B♭ Dmi B♭ Dmi
B♭ A A/C♯ Dmi
B♭ Dmi B♭ Dmi
B♭ A A/C♯ Dmi

Outline i–ii–V–i progressions with seventh arpeggios in each minor key through the cycle of 4ths. Start with A minor, then D minor, then G minor, C minor, F minor, etc. The first three arpeggios in the example start on the roots just to show the shapes, but then they switch by the shortest possible distance to any note in the next arpeggio, which should be your goal as soon as possible. The CD track is just an example; you should find your own daily tempo for all of these exercises. When in doubt, slow it down.

Track 37

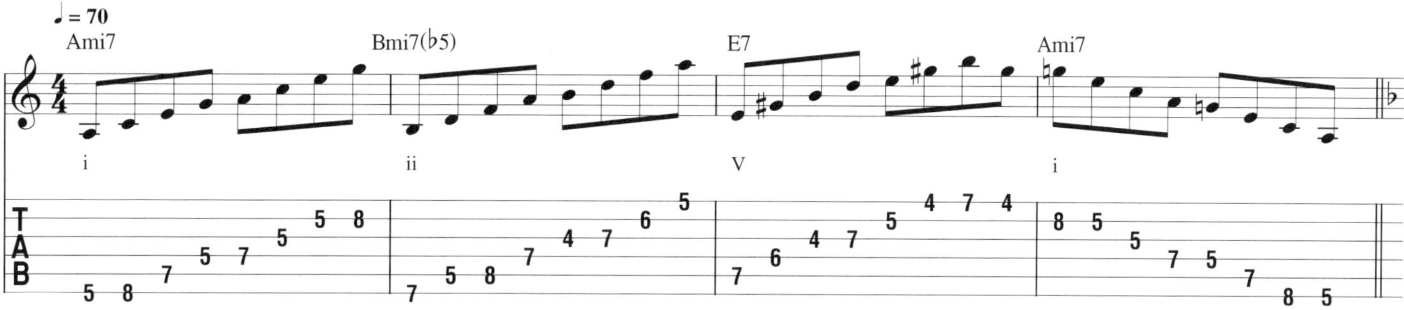


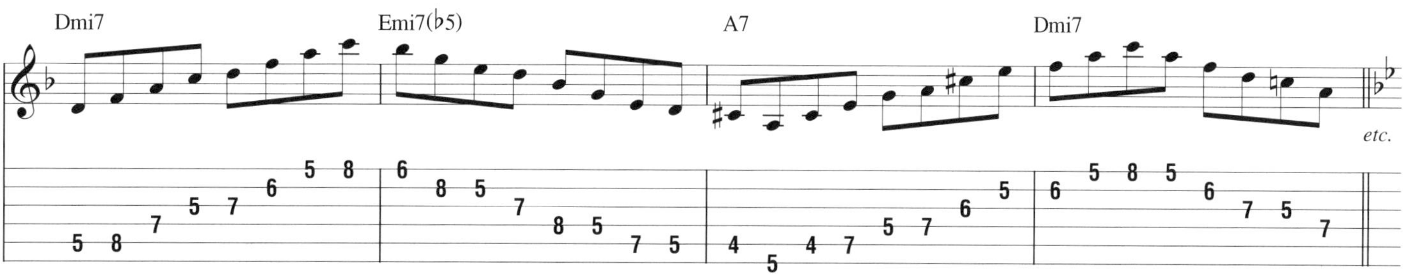


Cover up the answers below; find the possible key center(s) of these short minor progressions. Then check your analyses.

1. Gmi7(♭5)–C7–Fmi7
2. Gmi7–F–E♭
3. A♭mi7–B♭mi7–E♭mi7
4. F–Emi–Ami
5. G♭7–A♭mi7
6. D–E–F♯mi
7. E♭mi7–B♭mi7
8. Dmi–Emi7(♭5)–A7
9. Emi7–Bmi7–D–G
10. F♯mi7–C♯mi7–A–B7

**Answers:**

1. F minor
2. G minor
3. E♭ minor
4. A minor
5. A♭ minor
6. F♯ minor
7. E♭ minor or B♭ minor
8. D minor
9. E minor or B minor
10. C♯ minor

# 12 Modes

This chapter requires you to be pretty solid on material from Chapters 6–11: the major scale formula, intervals, harmonized scales and their chord qualities, key centers, and the relative major and minor concept.

I first learned about the modes from a great teacher who explained them clearly. (This was before the invention of indoor plumbing, but that's another story.) We played them; I paid close attention and thought I understood the subject at the time, but when I went home and tried it again, I was lost. I had to go back and relearn it a few times before it sank in, but when it did, I was elated. Here were gobs of possibilities for new sounds in my playing, opening up all at once!

My students report similar experiences, so if mode theory doesn't make sense or seem useful right away, take a break from it, then come back and go through it again. Talking with an experienced teacher who can demonstrate it in context and confirm that you are finding the modes and phrasing within them effectively will help.

In Chapter 11, we saw how starting the major scale on step 6 creates its relative minor, a natural minor scale. In addition to having a new scale, the chord or progression you were now playing over reflected a minor key center. You had to rephrase licks within the scale to fit (and musically help create) this new harmonic environment.

This principle applies to every note of the major scale—not just the 6th degree. Each degree of the major scale is the root of a mode, giving us seven modes in all. The modes share the five fingering patterns of the major scale. They use the same notes, yet they all sound as different from the major scale as does the natural minor scale.

You actually already know the two most important modes. The first mode, Ionian, is the same as the major scale, and the sixth mode, Aeolian, is the same as the natural minor scale, which we can get by playing the major scale from step 6.

The second mode, Dorian, is produced by playing the major scale from step 2. It corresponds with the minor ii chord of the harmonized scale, making Dorian a minor scale as well.

If you have a song that stays on a Dmi chord for a long time, you might first think to play the D natural minor scale. If instead you chose to play the D Dorian mode, you'd get it by playing the notes of the C major scale. The hard thing is to do that while remembering that you're still in D minor. Your phrasing should emphasize the tones of the Dmi chord, especially the root (D) for now. Even though you're playing the notes of the C major scale, you're not in the key of C at all—you're in D minor.

**D Dorian**

The same concept applies to the other modes. Each can be applied to at least one harmonic situation, which we'll learn to recognize so we can use the right mode.

## Finding the Modes

We'll first learn to play a mode by finding the major scale upon which it is based. We can call this the "parent" major scale.

Eventually you'll play the modes more as if they were separate scales with their own distinct spellings and sounds. With time you'll spend less time thinking about their parent major scales. Even the fingerings will feel different from the major scale (though they're not; they all share the same five patterns). However, learning them separately is making unnecessary work for yourself: seven modes times five patterns for each equals thirty-five new scale patterns to learn, when they're actually reiterations of the major scale. It's easier to apply the same five patterns you already know, reorienting yourself to center your phrases on the new root.

Memorize the order of the modes, with their numbers and Greek names. Mixolydian does not rhyme with *Nickelodeon.*

I Ionian
ii Dorian
iii Phrygian
IV Lydian
V Mixolydian
vi Aeolian
vii Locrian

When you have them memorized, you should be able to state the number of any mode or name the mode when you only have the number. Cover the page with your hand and test your knowledge.

## Find the Ionian

Your goal is to find the parent major scale (or Ionian mode) for any given mode on any given root. We can make it easy by breaking the process into steps. Memorize the steps (I suggest copying them down a few times), and run through them the same way every time you want a mode.

Let's say we want the G Lydian mode. (We'll get into *why* we want it after you know how to find it.)

1. Remember the mode number.
   Lydian is mode IV.

2. Assign the number to the root of the mode.
   G is IV.

3. Count down (or up) the **major scale formula** to *find the Ionian.* This is the parent major scale. For Lydian (IV), counting down is the shorter path.

   Counting Down:

   ? ← ← ←
   D E F♯ G
   I ii iii IV

   Counting Up:

   → → → → ?
   G A B C♯ D
   IV V vi vii VIII

4. Play the parent major scale, but from the mode root. Play the D major scale from G to G to get G Lydian.
   G A B C♯ D E F♯ G

Here are a few practice problems. Find these modes by following the four steps. The answers are below. Hide them until you're done.

1. B♭ Phrygian
2. D♯ Locrian
3. C Lydian
4. B Locrian
5. C Aeolian
6. F Mixolydian
7. C♯ Dorian
8. A♭ Dorian
9. E Ionian
10. A Lydian

**Answers:**

1. G♭ major from B♭ to B♭
2. E major from D♯ to D♯
3. G major from C to C
4. C major from B to B
5. E♭ major from C to C
6. B♭ major from F to F
7. B major from C♯ to C♯
8. G♭ major from A♭ to A♭
9. E major from E to E
10. E major from A to A

If that didn't go as expected, maybe you're not using the major scale formula: half steps from 3–4 and 7–8. Another common mistake is to make your mode "I" and start counting from there. Don't jump the gun; take it step by step at first.

## Using the Modes

When you can find the parent major scale for any mode, let's look at modes the other way: as unique scales, each with its own spelling. This will help us learn when to use each mode, because we want them to fit chords that contain the same notes (with a few exceptions that I'll point out).

| | | |
|---|---|---|
| I | Ionian | 1 2 3 4 5 6 7 8 |
| ii | Dorian | 1 2 ♭3 4 5 6 ♭7 8 |
| iii | Phrygian | 1 ♭2 ♭3 4 5 ♭6 ♭7 8 |
| IV | Lydian | 1 2 3 ♯4 5 6 7 8 |
| V | Mixolydian | 1 2 3 4 5 6 ♭7 8 |
| vi | Aeolian | 1 2 ♭3 4 5 ♭6 ♭7 8 |
| vii | Locrian | 1 ♭2 ♭3 4 ♭5 ♭6 ♭7 8 |

Check out the first column. Just like the 7th chord qualities of the harmonized major scale, we have major modes (uppercase) on I and IV, with a dominant mode on V. We have minor modes (lowercase) on ii, iii, and vi. On step vii, we have a mode with a ♭3 and ♭5 that would fit a diminished triad or a mi7(♭5) chord. Each mode has a note that further distinguishes it from others of its basic type (major or minor) that will help us decide when to use it.

| | | Chord It Fits | Distinguishing Note(s) | Musical Effect |
|---|---|---|---|---|
| I | Ionian | Major 7 | 4, 7 | Major |
| ii | Dorian | minor 7 | 6 | Jazzy Minor |
| iii | Phrygian | minor 7 | ♭2 | Gypsy Minor |
| IV | Lydian | Major 7 | ♯4 | Ambiguous |
| V | Mixolydian | Dominant 7 | ♭7 | Funk or Blues |
| vi | Aeolian | mi7 | ♭6 | Natural Minor |
| vii | Locrian | mi7(♭5) | ♭5 | Dissonant, Unstable |

When a single chord is repeated for many measures (a "static" chord), you can choose a mode from those that fit the chord type based on its musical or emotional effect. The terms used in the last column are just superficial generalizations to help you learn, not truly representative of all that the modes are capable of. When multiple chords are present, the notes they contain will usually dictate one mode choice. In a song with frequent chord changes, fit as many chords as possible with one mode before you are forced to change to another one.

## Major-Sounding Modes

The major-sounding modes are Ionian, Lydian, and Mixolydian. Each contains a major 3rd.

On a static ma7 chord, we can add variety with the sound of the Lydian mode instead of Ionian. With its unstable ♯4th degree, Lydian can sound wistful, ambient and floating, or even comical in some situations (it's used in some TV cartoon themes). In comparison, the Ionian mode is heavier, more majestic, and grounded in *tonality*: the sensation that one note is the root above all others. Use Ionian on major key centers.

Because it is built on step IV, Lydian takes away the sensation that the chord it is being played over is a I, or tonic chord. We should use Lydian from the root of *any* ma7 chord that is not the I chord, unless we're changing keys to the root of that chord. Sometimes non-diatonic ma7 chords are inserted into a progression almost at random to add an element of unpredictability without changing keys. We want to "float" over these chords with Lydian until the strong tonality returns. Here we play C Ionian over a ii–V in C, switch to A♭ Lydian for the "surprise" A♭maj7 (♭VIma7), then back to C for the I.

| C Ionian | — | | | A♭ Lydian | — | C Ionian |
|---|---|---|---|---|---|---|
| **Dmi7** | | **G7** | | **A♭ma7** | | **Cma7** |
| ii | — | V | — | ♭VI | — | I |

The only mode in the list that contains all the tones in a dominant 7th chord is Mixolydian. As an example, if an E7 funk groove were played, we could use E Mixolydian over it. If we played some minor pentatonic or blues licks, that would be OK, too, but those scales have notes that technically "clash" with the chord (though most of us born in the last hundred years are used to this particular dissonance by now).

A "modal progression" is frequently used as an alternative to a major or minor key center. A Mixolydian modal progression is the most commonly used alternative to major keys. The harmonized Mixolydian scale is the same as harmonized major from step V. Here's a direct comparison of Mixolydian to Ionian.

| | | | | | | | |
|---|---|---|---|---|---|---|---|
| Ionian: | Ima7 | iimi7 | iiimi7 | IVma7 | V7 | vimi7 | viimi7(♭5) |
| Mixolydian: | I7 | iimi7 | iiimi7(♭5) | IVma7 | vmi7 | vimi7 | ♭VIIma7 |

Notice they have the same chords on steps ii, IV, and vi. On I, iii, and V they share roots but have different chord types. The chords on step vii in Ionian and ♭VII in Mixolydian have different roots (though the rest of their notes are identical). This is all caused by the presence of the ♭7 in Mixolydian, a difference of one note that makes a big difference in sound and feel. Typical Mixolydian progressions feature the ♭VII major triad or ma7 chord after the I major triad.

G Mixolydian

| **G** | **Fma7** |
|---|---|
| I | ♭VIIma7 |

I major followed by v minor is another common Mixolydian chord move.

G Mixolydian

| **G** | **Dmi** | **F** | **C** |
|---|---|---|---|
| I | vmi | ♭VII | IV |

In a modal progression, the chords must be arranged in a way that helps emphasize the tonal center. Put the I or I7 at the beginning of a phrase. (Measure 1 can also sound like the *end* of the section if it repeats.) If you put IV at the beginning of the phrase you risk replacing the Mixolydian sound with the parent major key. Playing the chords from the previous example in a different order puts us in the key of C major.

C major

| **C** | **F** | **Dmi** | **G** |
|---|---|---|---|
| I | IV | ii | V |

Suppose a progression starts with a I major triad, then moves to IV, ii, and/or vi. By comparing major with Mixolydian harmony we know these chords do not nail down the tonality either way; none of them contains the 7th degree of the overall key. It looks like a major key center on the surface, but we can play Mixolydian to get that wrenching ♭7th in there. Of course, it has to fit the style of the song.

B♭ Mixolydian

| **B♭** | **E♭** |
|---|---|
| I | IV |

A less-common alternative to a major key center is a Lydian modal progression. Learn to spot a Ima7 to II, or II7, progression as a likely place to use the Lydian mode.

G Lydian

| **Gma7** | **A** |
|---|---|
| Ima7 | II |

The distinguishing note of the Lydian mode, the ♯4th degree, can be added above the 7th (making it a ♯11th) of a ma7 chord to instantly impart the Lydian flavor. A chord spelled with the "ma7(♭5)" name is nearly the same thing (♯4 = ♭5). Play the Lydian mode over ma7 chords or major triads with ♯11 or ♭5.

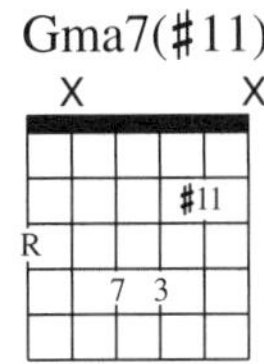


## Analysis Review

Working from the Roman numerals, write out the major-sounding progressions presented so far in this chapter, in the keys of E, B♭, D, F, and C.

## Minor-Sounding Modes

The minor-sounding modes are Dorian, Phrygian, Aeolian, and, to the extent that it shares the ♭3 and ♭7, Locrian.

Previously, we considered D Dorian instead of D Aeolian on a static Dmi chord. The difference between the two is the presence of the major 6th in the Dorian mode. It's a lighter, slightly jazzier, and also funkier, bluesier, and more down-home countrified sound. What can I say? I like that note. Most old-school blues and rock players seem to prefer Dorian instead of Aeolian when a progression is open to either.

Comparing Dorian to Aeolian, we have the same chords on I, ♭III, and v. As long as the 6th degree is not present in any of the chords of a minor progression, we're free to choose either mode, or mix both together, playing licks that include the 6 and ♭6.

| | | | | | | | |
|---|---|---|---|---|---|---|---|
| Aeolian: | imi7 | iimi7(♭5) | ♭IIIma7 | ivmi7 | vmi7 | ♭VIma7 | ♭VII7 |
| Dorian: | imi7 | iimi7 | ♭IIIma7 | IV7 | vmi7 | vimi7(♭5) | ♭VIIma7 |

Santana's guitar melodies on "Oye Como Va" are a good example of pure Dorian on a strictly Dorian modal progression: Ami7–D7 (i–IV7). Hendrix also used Dorian frequently. Like many players, he often "forced" its minor sound over dominant chords and major triads with great results in the same way minor pentatonic and blues scales are used in roots styles like blues and rockabilly.

The major 6th in Dorian usually clashes unfavorably with iimi7(♭5), iv, ♭VIma7, and ♭VII7 chords in diatonic minor progressions; for these, Aeolian is the right choice for playing with a key-center approach. You can always just shift from Aeolian to the Dorian mode if you like its sound when a i, ♭III, or v chord appears in a diatonic minor progression. You're only changing one note. Just be sure you're not leaning on that 6th when a chord containing the ♭6th comes up.

Following are some typical minor progressions that we should learn to recognize quickly so we can play the right minor mode. We want to see if any chord in the progression contains either the ♭6th (requiring Aeolian) or the major 6th (requiring Dorian). We'll spell the chords, put all the notes in alphabetical order, then convert them to numbers in relation to the tonic minor chord of the progression.

On a minor progression that has a ♭VI major chord (down two whole steps from the i), use Aeolian. This is one of the most common minor-key movements in rock.

| | |
|---|---|
| i | ♭VI |
| **Dmi** | **B♭** |
| (D–F–A) | (B♭–D–F) |

When we put all the notes in alphabetical order, there is enough to imply Aeolian.

| D | | F | | A | B♭ | | D |
|---|---|---|---|---|---|---|---|
| 1 | 2 | ♭3 | 4 | 5 | ♭6 | ♭7 | 8 |

A minor i chord with a major or dominant IV chord makes up the classic Dorian situation. The major 3rd of the IV chord is also the major 6th of the i.

| i | IV |
|---|---|
| **Dmi** | **G** |
| (D–F–A) | (G–B–D) |

| D | | F | G | A | B | | D |
|---|---|---|---|---|---|---|---|
| 1 | 2 | ♭3 | 4 | 5 | 6 | ♭7 | 8 |

If the iv chord is minor, we're back in the Aeolian mode.

| i | iv |
|---|---|
| **Dmi** | **Gmi** |
| (D–F–A) | (G–B♭–D) |

If there's a iimi7(♭5) chord, the progression is Aeolian, though that ii is almost always followed by V7, which can take D harmonic minor in this key.

| iimi7(♭5) | V7 | imi7 | |
|---|---|---|---|
| **Emi7(♭5)** | **A7** | **Dmi7** | **Dmi7** |
| (E–G–B♭–D) | (A–C♯–E–G) | (D–F–A–C) | |

Aeolian

| D | E | F | G | A | B♭ | C | D |
|---|---|---|---|---|---|---|---|
| 1 | 2 | ♭3 | 4 | 5 | ♭6 | ♭7 | 8 |

Harmonic Minor

| D | E | F | G | A | B♭ | C♯ | D |
|---|---|---|---|---|---|---|---|
| 1 | 2 | ♭3 | 4 | 5 | ♭6——— | 7 | 8 |

Suppose we have a ii chord that is not a mi7(♭5) but instead just minor. Spell the notes in the chords and you'll see the difference is B instead of B♭. This is the major 6th of D, so we play Dorian.

| i | ii |
|---|---|
| **Dmi7** | **Emi7** |
| (D–F–A–C) | E–G–B–D) |

Dorian

| D | E | F | G | A | B | C |
|---|---|---|---|---|---|---|
| 1 | 2 | ♭3 | 4 | 5 | 6 | ♭7 |

Phrygian is a darker and more unstable choice over a static minor chord, with its ♭2nd degree creating tension. Phrygian gets that clichè flamenco sound when used by itself. When it is sparingly applied in the right situations, it doesn't stick out so much, but instead just takes the music down to a thoughtful, brooding place, so you can then start things moving up again—a nice effect. On the other hand, you can just hammer away at it if you want to be evil.

Finding the Phrygian mode at the right time is hard because it's not as common as other situations. Watch out for a minor chord followed by a major chord a half step higher, or by a minor chord a whole step below.

| i | ♭II | i | ♭viimi |
|---|---|---|---|
| **Dmi** | **E♭** | **Dmi** | **Cmi** |
| (D–F–A) | (E♭–G–B♭) | | (C–E♭–G) |

| D | E♭ | F | G | A | B♭ | C | D |
|---|---|---|---|---|---|---|---|
| 1 | ♭2 | ♭3 | 4 | 5 | ♭6 | ♭7 | 8 |

## Analysis Review

Working from the Roman numerals, write out the minor progressions presented in this chapter, in the keys of G minor, E minor, B♭ minor, F minor, and C minor.

## The Locrian Mode

This mode is in its own category. Locrian is played on the mi7(♭5) chord, which, containing a ♭2 and a ♭5, is so unstable that it cannot be "tonicized." You can't make it into a tonic chord; it always wants to move someplace else. Attempts to tonicize it require the listener to accept a lot of tension, and usually instead of a discrete harmonic entity give the impression of Phrygian with a ♭5 added as an alteration.

The mi7(♭5) chord is almost always the ii chord in a minor key center. Using Aeolian over the entire key center will give you Locrian on the ii automatically, though you should learn to start this mode from a tone of the chord it appears on, rather than a tone of the i chord.

## Practicing the Modes

I suggest initially memorizing at least one pattern of Dorian, Mixolydian, and Aeolian (pattern 4 is a good choice), so that you can grab these important modes without thinking of the parent major scale. This way you can jump right in without a delay in your playing. After you've started playing in that pattern, in a few seconds you'll remember the parent major scale for the mode you're in (recognizing which pattern number of major scale you're in at the time will help). Then you can start moving up or down the fretboard if necessary, using the other patterns of the major scale that are equal to the mode you want. Eventually the parent scale reference will become less necessary.

To get the modes in your ears and under your fingers, play over the following short practice progressions. A droning bass note reinforces the root of the mode in each example. Every note in the mode is included somewhere within the chords, with emphasis placed on the distinguishing note. In the first example, the chords are C (C–E–G), G/C (C–G–B–D), and F/C (C–F–A). If you put all the notes in these chords in alphabetical order, the C Ionian mode is spelled: C–D–E–F–G–A–B.

Over each chord track, the correct mode is first played in eighth notes, followed by a bit of improvisation to emphasize its sound. After checking that you have the right notes, dial out my improvisation and try some of your own. Then start again, re-recording the chord tracks in other keys.

Track 38

**C Ionian (C major from C to C)**

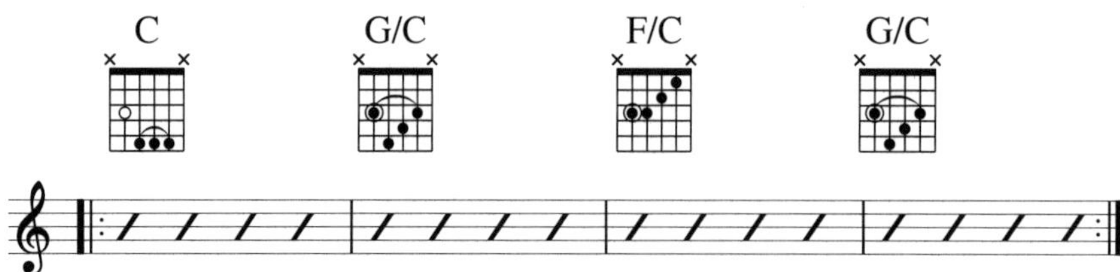

Track 39

**C Dorian (B♭ major from C to C)**

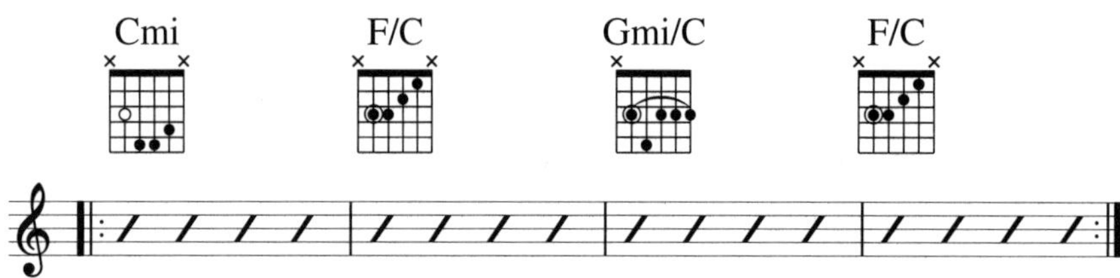

Track 40

**C Phrygian (A♭ major from C to C)**

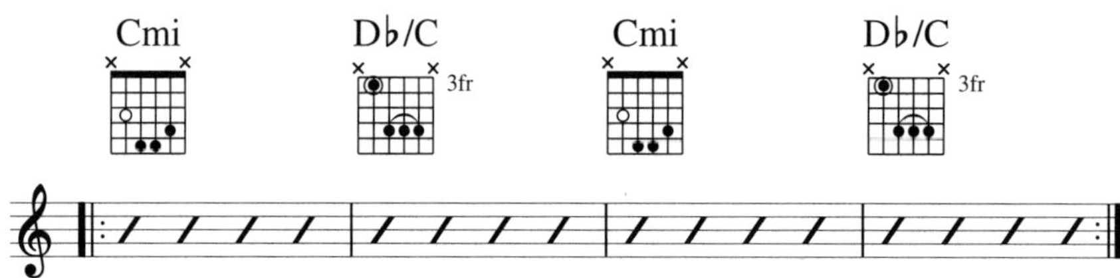

Track 41

**C Lydian (G major from C to C)**

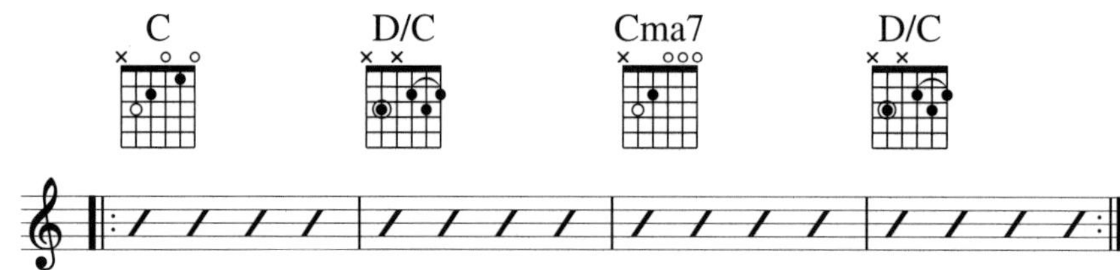

Track 42

**C Mixolydian (F major from C to C)**

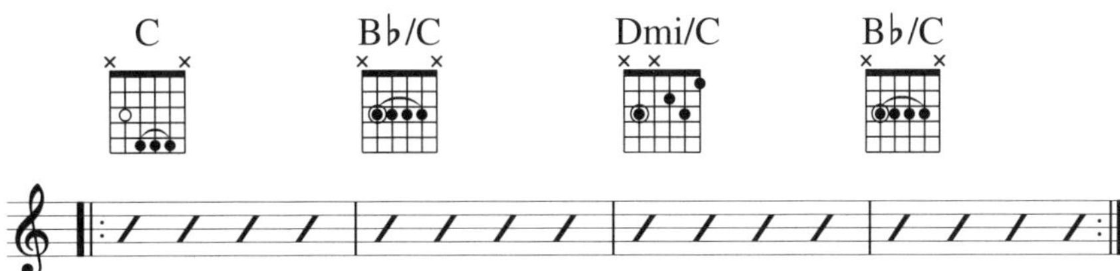

Track 43

**C Aeolian (E♭ major from C to C)**

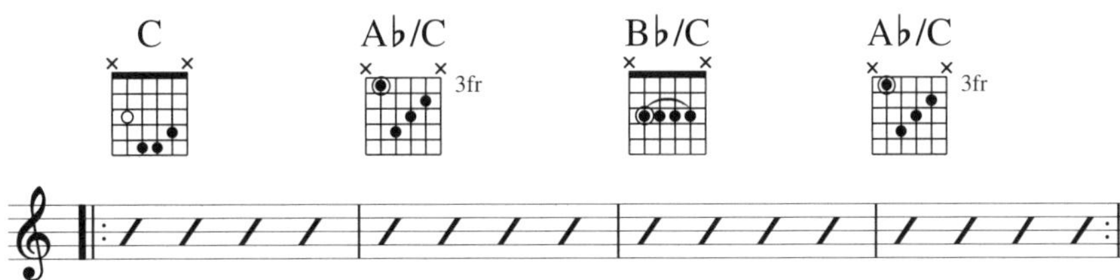


Most chord progressions can be categorized as either tonal or modal. Tonal progressions are major or minor key centers, where it's pretty obvious which chord is acting as I. In modal progressions, it's sometimes not always so clear to the listener which chord is the I, which may be part of their appeal. As long as the melody has some repetitive, easy-to-follow phrases, the tonic does not need emphasis, and the ear gets a break from tonal orientation. Not only can we choose which mode(s) to use over a particular chord or progression, occasionally we get to decide (or argue about) which note is the tonic!

The next time you happen to hear "Sweet Home Alabama," notice that most of the song is a simple repeated three-chord progression (D–C–G), where the vocalist seems to treat D as the I, staying entirely within D Dorian with his melody and returning to the note D with nearly every phrase, making the progression a I–♭VII–IV in D. However, the long guitar solo sticks to the G tonality over exactly the same chords, making the progression a V–IV–I in G major. Because we're all accustomed to hearing these chords interpreted either way, the perceived key center changes just on the basis of what's happening in the lead instrument (or voice).

## Listening

You can see that mode theory is a broad subject worthy of in-depth study. Below are just a few suggested listening examples that feature extended modal sections that should be easy for you to identify. Learn any easy melodies and progressions you hear in these songs. Often modal components are used to provide variety as bridges (a *bridge* is a section intended to contrast with the verses and choruses) or solo sections of songs.

### Dorian

- Miles Davis, "So What"—This archetypal modal jazz progression moves from D Dorian to E♭ Dorian.

### Lydian

- Joe Satriani, "Flying in a Blue Dream"—C Lydian and A♭ Lydian modes are used in the melody.

**Mixolydian**

- Jeff Beck, "Freeway Jam"—Beck uses pure Mixolydian for the main melody and mixes it with minor pentatonic in his solos. (Check out the Phrygian-flavored keyboard fills in the fadeout.)
- Allman Brothers, "Jessica"—While the acoustic rhythm guitar hints at Mixolydian, Dickey Betts and Duane Allman use an ambiguous A hexatonic (six-note) major scale (1–2–3–4–5–6) on the main melody, harmonizing it with major pentatonic (1–2–3–5–6). Betts switches to G major and then A Mixolydian for the bridge melody.

## What, Me Worry?

If you have a series of chords that define a key center—for instance, a I–vi–ii–V—you're better off not changing modes to fit each chord. Without changing scales, you will automatically get Ionian over the I chord, Aeolian on the vi chord, Dorian on the ii, and Mixolydian on the V. Jumping into alternate modes could make your playing sound choppy and disconnected. In many cases, a nice, logical melody with a few strategically placed chord tones within the parent major or minor scale is the best way to go. We'll work on this in Part III with chord-tone targeting exercises.

In the case of rock, blues, and country, often your choice of notes is only partly dictated by the chords, which may be triads, power (1–5) chords, single bass notes, or riffs. Minor and major pentatonics, Mixolydian, Dorian, and the blues scale (1–♭3–4–♭5–5–♭7) are frequently mixed together or used one after another as a kind of "Mixobluesian" übermode over major triads, dominant 7th chords, power chords, droning bass notes, or riffs, where only the tonic note is set in stone. Any attempt to get analytical over grooves in these roots styles can sound inauthentic, or worse, just plain uncool.

Even when using a high proportion of non-diatonic notes, however, any style of soloing benefits from tone targeting. There will be times when the target notes are in neither the chord nor the diatonic scale of the piece—an idea we saw with the blues in Chapter 2.

Finally, there is the option of forcing a "wrong" mode over chords. It's not something I usually recommend except in the case I've already mentioned: using Dorian (or minor pentatonic or the blues scale) on major triads or dominant 7th chords. As an example of something not to do, playing any other mode we've studied except Ionian or Lydian on a Ima7 chord usually sounds bad to me, as does any major-sounding mode over a tonic minor chord. Try anything; but when in doubt, leave it out.

# Extensions

The common-practice exceptions to the rules of chord extension (and alteration) can be hard to remember. You may read this chapter and play the extensions without memorizing all the "irregularities" at first, then refer back to this chapter when you need to. We can't leave any of these little rules out, however, because eventually you'll need them. We spare no expense here at Acme Extensions, Inc.

Extensions (sometimes called *tension notes*) are 9th, 11th, or 13th intervals added to a chord or arpeggio. Extended chords may be written into the music, or they may be substituted for seventh chords or triads as the player sees fit. Here are some extended chord symbols:

B9 F♯mi11 A♭ma13 Cmi9(♭5)

All extensions up to and including the highest one stated in the chord name are theoretically included, though sometimes this is impossible because the full chord exceeds the six-note limit of the guitar (or is unplayable by the four fingers and thumb). It also might sound clearer or less muddy with some of the notes removed. In practice, the extension listed in the name should be added to the seventh chord. Any lower extensions are optional. Usually the extensions are played higher in the chord than the basic 1, 3, 5, and 7, though there are many exceptions in chord-voicing practice, to better fit melodies, or to make the extended chord playable within the limits of the guitar.

When playing an extended arpeggio, you are free to include any of its notes in any octave, but if you play the basic chord tones and all three extensions in the same octave, you've turned it into a seven-note scale (sometimes called the *chord scale*) that is exactly related to the extended chord. That scale will be useful to know, but to keep its distinct quality the arpeggio is played in numeric order: 1–3–5–7–9–11–13 (though the sequence may be started on any note, and some notes may be omitted). Use the reverse order when practicing a descending extended arpeggio: 13–11–9–7–5–3–1, starting on any note.

Besides the basic shapes here, there are endless permutations of chord tones and extensions, some spanning multiple positions and incorporating open strings. We'll start by learning two extended chord voicings and two basic positional patterns of extended minor, major, and dominant arpeggios. Eventually you'll want to learn all five patterns of each type of extended arpeggio. A good way is to count up to the extended notes in each pattern using the scale as a reference, then make your own diagrams. Buying a book of all possible arpeggio shapes won't help as much as drawing them on your own.

## Minor

A minor 7th arpeggio with the basic chord tones and the 9th, 11th, and 13th all in the same octave is equal to the Dorian mode. Again, these are the notes used, but we'll spread them out over two octaves in the extended arpeggio.

(Dmi9, Dmi11) Dmi13: 1, ♭3, 5, ♭7, 9, 11, 13

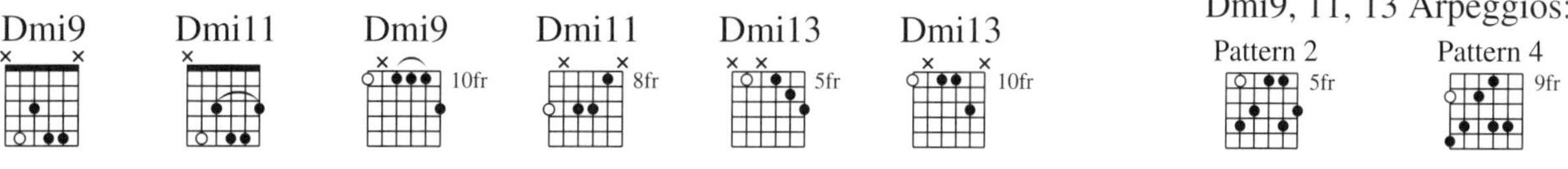


The mi13 chord is not as commonly used as the other extended minor types: mi9, mi11.

## Major

A major 7th arpeggio with the basic chord tones and the 9th, 11th, and 13th included in the same octave equals the major scale (or Ionian mode). The 11th is usually omitted when extending the major chord, but you can include the 11th in the arpeggio.

(Cma9, Cma11) Cma13: 1, 3, 5, 7, 9, 11, 13

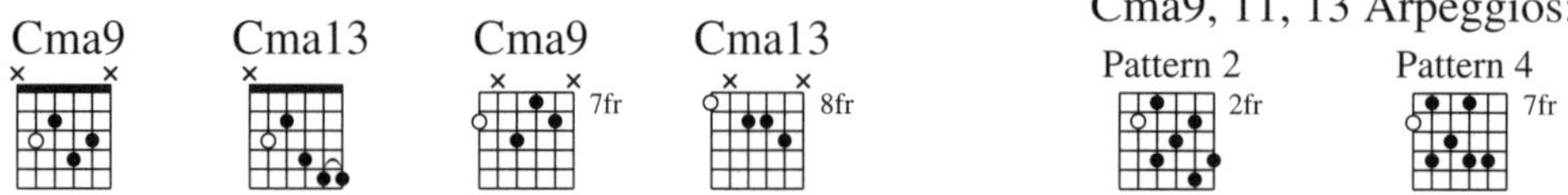


Here's where it starts to get hairy. The 11th interval is the compound equivalent of the perfect 4th. The 4th and 3rd can clash in a way that is not always desirable when played together. This means major and dominant chords need special consideration when being extended up to or beyond the 11th. In a ma7 chord, the clash is doubly bad, as the 4th also forms an extremely dissonant tritone with the major 7th of the chord. The clash is not a problem in an arpeggio, because the notes are not simultaneous, but it's a real concern when playing a chord. However, if you've changed a chord, the arpeggio would need the same alteration in order to fit it.

Often, the 11th is augmented (raised by a half step) when extending a major or dominant chord, avoiding the clash with the major 3rd. The symbol ♯11 is written on each chord name where this note is used.

Cma9(♯11): 1, 3, 5, 7, 9, ♯11

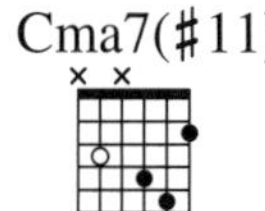


If the 9th, ♯11th, and 13th were included in the same octave with the root, 3rd, 5th, and 7th of a ma7th arpeggio, you'd have the Lydian mode. Again, those are the notes, but for melodic practice we spread the notes out over two octaves.

Cma13(♯11): 1, 3, 5, 7, 9, ♯11, 13

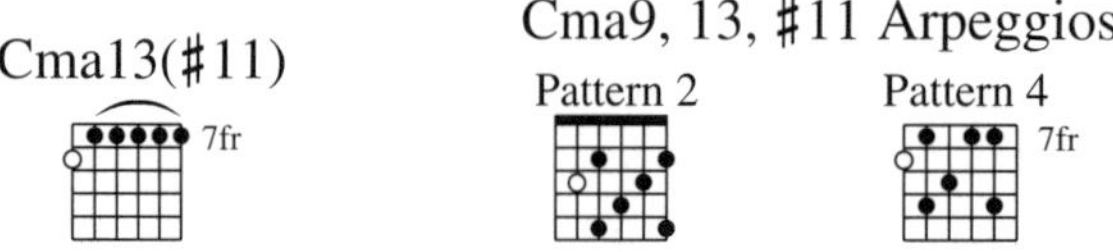

## Dominant

A dominant 7th arpeggio with the basic chord tones and the 9th, 11th, and 13th in the same octave equals the Mixolydian mode. The clashing 3rd and 11th are here also, though dominant chords are often a place we expect to feel more tension.

(G9, G11) G13: 1, 3, 5, ♭7, 9, 11, 13

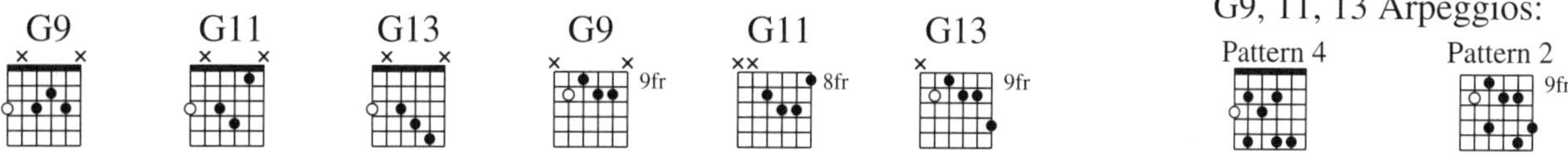


When the 9th, ♯11th, and 13th are included in the same octave with the 1–3–5–♭7 of a dominant 7th arpeggio, you have a scale called *Lydian dominant*, or just *Lydian ♭7*. (Lydian ♭7 is the fifth mode of the *melodic minor scale*, a fact you can ignore for now.)

G13(♯11): 1, 3, 5, ♭7, 9, ♯11, 13

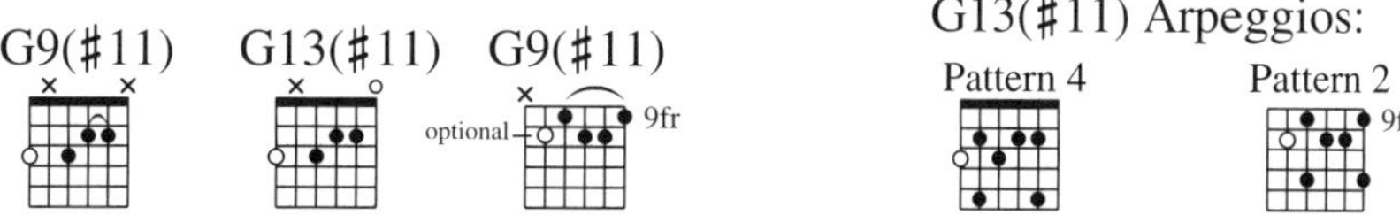


Besides raising the 11th, you can also simply omit it altogether to avoid having those two notes clash when constructing a major 13th or dominant 13th chord.

Omitting the 11th
G13: 1, 3, 5, ♭7, 9, 13
Cma13: 1, 3, 5, 7, 9, 13

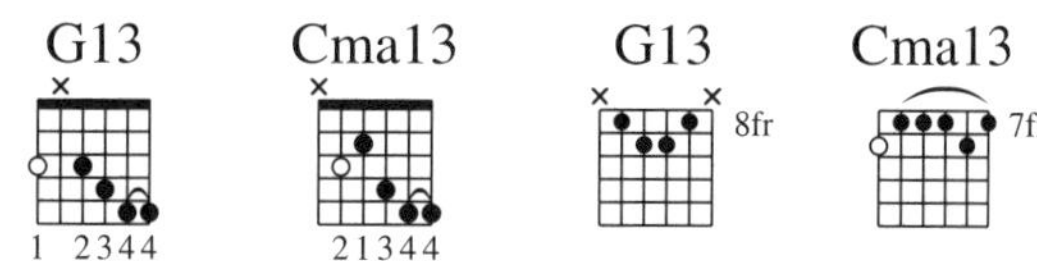


You can also omit the 3rd of the dominant 11th or 13th chord. Other names for these are "7sus," "9sus," and "13sus."

Omitting the 3rd
G11: 1, 5, ♭7, 9, 11
G13sus: 1, 5, ♭7, 9, 11, 13

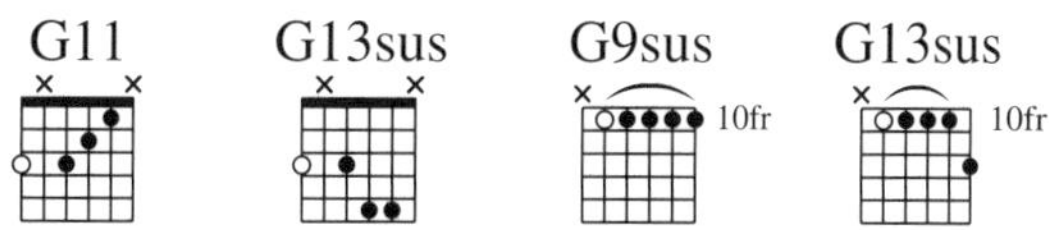

When soloing over a chord with the 3rd or 11th omitted, you can include the 3rd. You can include the perfect 4th (or 11th) if the chord is a diatonic I or V. If the chord is the IV in the key, the ♯4th is the better choice because it is the 7th of the overall key. (This means you're playing Lydian over that chord.)

On *non-diatonic* chords, choose the 11th (perfect or augmented) that fits the key center. In other words, play the diatonic note that is either type of 4th for the chord. For major chords, this usually means to decide between Lydian or Ionian, with the preference going to Lydian. For non-diatonic dominant chords, the choice is often between Mixolydian and Lydian ♭7. The choice is also influenced by the style of music. The ♯11 has a jazzier flavor, and though technically right, can sound out of place in some music.

## Sixth Chords

These are not seventh or extended chords but another category that it is important to know. We're covering them now because they have some modal implications.

### Major 6th

Spelled 1–3–5–6, the major sixth chord is substituted for a major triad or a major seventh chord, and when soloing in a diatonic context like a jazz standard should take Ionian or Lydian. (Don't use Mixolydian, in other words.) In rock, blues, or country solos, you can use Mixolydian (or again, Dorian, for a twangy taste) over a I6 chord if you would have done so over a triad or dominant seventh chord in the same place.

### Minor 6th

The minor sixth chord is a minor triad with a major 6th interval added (never a minor 6th interval!): 1–♭3–5–6. The correct scale to play over this chord is usually the Dorian mode.

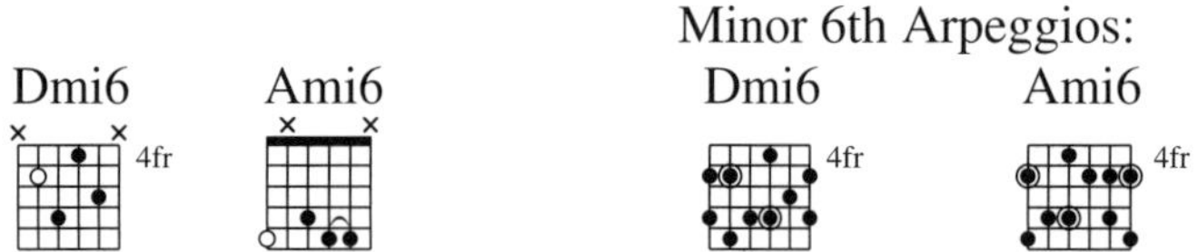


Besides using a metronome in eighth notes, ascending and descending in the five patterns through various keys, extended arpeggios may also be practiced in groups of two, three, or four, as we did with triads and seventh arpeggios.

## Alterations

Extensions are always major or perfect unless otherwise stated in the chord name. Though the word *altered* can be used to describe any note that's been changed, *altered extensions* are ones that are not major or perfect when looked at only in relation to the root of the chord. Extending some diatonic chords produces altered extensions (especially in minor keys), but these notes are in the key center, which means there's nothing really "changed" about them. In fact, using unaltered extensions on some chords can produce notes that clash with the key center.

Besides being altered for the purpose of keeping in the key center, at other times extensions are altered just because we like the sound.

The V chord in a minor key is the most obvious place alterations are used. This chord may draw its notes from the natural or harmonic-minor scale of the related i chord, producing ♭9, ♯9, and ♯5 (equal to ♭13) extensions.

Here are dominant arpeggio patterns with these altered extensions, along with some chord voicings. These may sound strange at first; follow each with an Fmi chord and it will all make sense.

C7(♭9)(♯9)(♭13): 1, 3, 5, ♭7, ♭9, ♯9, ♭13

Altered Dominant Chords:

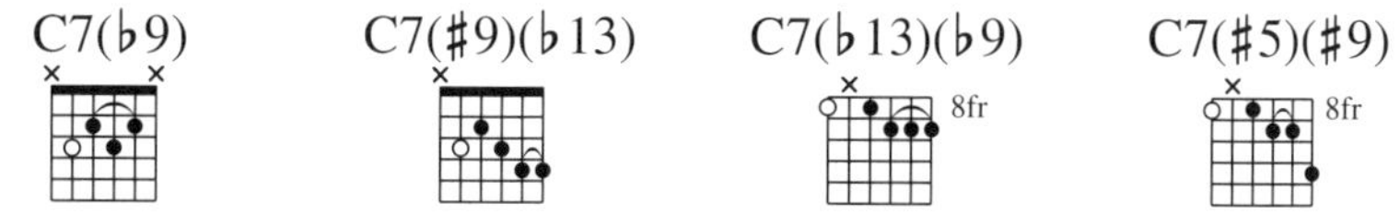

C7(♭9) C7(♯9)(♭13) C7(♭13)(♭9) 8fr C7(♯5)(♯9) 8fr

Altered Dominant Arpeggios:

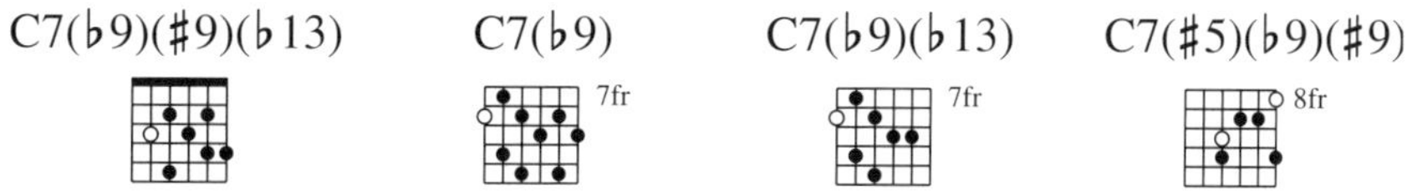

C7(♭9)(♯9)(♭13) C7(♭9) 7fr C7(♭9)(♭13) 7fr C7(♯5)(♭9)(♯9) 8fr

Dominant chords provide the most freedom to go nuts with alteration. Any combination of natural and altered 5ths and/or 9ths is possible, depending on factors like the surrounding chords and the style of the song. Each combination of extensions creates its own scalar implications, including the *altered*, *dominant diminished*, and *whole-tone* scales, which we won't cover here; they're best left to a jazz method book. However, no matter what you may encounter, the golden rule applies: the chord tones are never wrong. The more extended a chord is, the fewer actual choices you have to make when soloing over it.

I suggest starting off learning just one or two shapes of a dominant 7♯5(♭9)(♯9) arpeggio so that you'll be ready for Part III.

# Modal Interchange, Secondary Dominants, and Modulation

## Modal Interchange

In Chapter 11 we learned about the relative major/minor concept. Two scales are said to be relative if they share the same notes but start on different ones. *Parallel* scales are scales that share the same root. For instance, the *parallel minor* scale of D major is D minor. The *parallel major* scale of A minor is A major. The same principle may be applied to modes, or most any type of scale; any scale has parallels with the same root but different quality.

*Modal interchange* is the use of a chord derived from the harmony of a parallel scale or mode. The overall key center is not considered to have changed. Here are some examples of modal interchange.

1.

| **C** | **C** | **G** | **G** | **F** | **Fmi** | **C** | **C** |
|---|---|---|---|---|---|---|---|
| C major | | | | | C minor | C major | |

2.

| **E** | **E** | **G♯mi** | **A** | **C** | **D** | **E** | **E** |
|---|---|---|---|---|---|---|---|
| E major | | | | E minor | | E major | |

3.

| **Gmi** | **F** | **E♭** | **C/E** | **F** | **C** | **D** | **D** |
|---|---|---|---|---|---|---|---|
| G Aeolian | | | G Dorian | | | G harmonic minor | |

When soloing over progressions containing modal interchange, switch to the parallel scale over the non-diatonic chord. At first you should practice emphasizing the chord tones that are different from the original key by making them target notes. Once you're comfortable with the change, you may decide to downplay it by using a target note that is common to both the non-diatonic chord and the original scale.

It's usually not OK to ignore modal interchange chords entirely. For instance, in Example 1 above, continuing to play the C major scale over the Fmi chord could find you hitting an A note, which will clash. It should be an A♭ instead.

There's an exception to the "you-can't-ignore-it" rule. If you are already superimposing Dorian, the blues scale, or a minor pentatonic scale over a major tonality, as we've discussed, your scale will usually (sort of) fit any chords borrowed from the parallel minor key—yet another reason this approach is so popular. It doesn't provide much variety, but it's easy and has that rock 'n' roll attitude.

## Secondary Dominants

Degree V in a key is called the *dominant*; a chord built on this note is usually dominant in quality. In minor keys, there is also a dominant chord on the ♭VII7.

Sometimes other chords with the dominant quality are inserted into a progression. Their effect is to create a very short sensation of a new key center based on the chord a 5th lower. That chord is said to be *tonicized.* The dominant chord that's doing the tonicizing is a *secondary dominant*, and is referred to as the "V of" that chord—for instance V/ii. Here, Ami is replaced by A7 in the key of C, giving the progression a little more momentum toward the Dmi chord.

| C | Ami | Dmi | G7 |
|---|---|---|---|
| I | vi | ii | V |

becomes:

| C | A7 | Dmi | G7 |
|---|---|---|---|
| I | V/ii | ii | V |

A secondary dominant does not have to be followed by its expected resolution. The example below is an example of a non-resolving secondary dominant:

| C | A7 | F | G7 |
|---|---|---|---|
| I | V/ii | IV | V |

In a major key there are five possible secondary dominants. Here they are in C:

| | |
|---|---|
| V/ii | A7 (resolves to Dmi) |
| V/iii | B7 (resolves to Emi) |
| V/IV | C7 (resolves to F) |
| V/V | D7 (resolves to G) |
| V/vi | E7 (resolves to Ami) |

F7 often appears in the key of C but is usually just considered a blues convention, not what we call *functional harmony* (a chord with an expected resolution up a 4th or down a 5th.) The blues scale of the overall key is a good scale choice on the IV7 chord.

First approaching them as real key centers, you can use Mixolydian over a secondary dominant that tonicizes a major or dominant chord. In C major, you'd switch to D Mixolydian over a D7 (V/V).

| C major | D Mixo | C major | |
|---|---|---|---|
| **C** | **D7** | **G** | **F** |
| I | V/V | V | IV |

Over a secondary dominant that tonicizes a minor chord, you can play the harmonic minor scale of the tonicized chord. This would mean over B7 in the key of C, you'd play E harmonic minor.

| C major | | E harmonic minor | | C major | | | |
|---|---|---|---|---|---|---|---|
| **C** | **Dmi** | **B7** | **Emi** | **F** | **Emi** | **Dmi** | **G7** |
| I | ii | V/iii | iii | IV | iii | ii | V |

Thinking in terms of just chord tones is especially useful when soloing over secondary-dominant chords. Since often the chord only appears for one measure or less, it's smoother not to think about an entirely new scale to fit it. Instead, you can just find the notes in the non-diatonic chord that are different from the original key and practice using them as target tones; the result sounds like a modified version of the original scale. In the previous example, you'd use the C major scale throughout, with D changed to D♯ and F changed to F♯ over the B7 chord. The notes are the same with either approach.

As with modal interchange, once you're comfortable with the change, you may decide to downplay it by using a target note that is common to both the non-diatonic chord and the original scale. In the previous example, playing G over the B7 would give you the 5th of the key center but a nice ♯5 on the V/iii chord.

The inspired-primitivist option of sticking with a blues or pentatonic scale over an entire progression is not as acceptable with secondary dominants as it is with modal interchange. For instance, playing the E♭ from the C minor pentatonic scale over an E7 (V/vi) in the key of C is likely to make your skin crawl.

In general, using chord tones in the context of the overall key works well over all non-diatonic chords of short duration. Some really good guitar players (Jeff Beck and Robben Ford spring to mind) make it a point to find one note from the blues or minor scale of the overall key that is also a 7th or an extension of the chord of the moment and build a lick that uses it, for the best of both worlds.

## Modulation

Modulation is a change of key, requiring us to completely shift to a new scale in the melody or solo. In a true key change, the root of the old key should be replaced by the new one in the listener's mind. This will happen if the new key is sustained long enough, or if it is emphasized by a strong chord move—say, V–I in the new key. If this doesn't happen, think of any non-diatonic chords as temporary tonicizing in the same old key, and keep the same tonic in mind in your phrasing. The difference is mainly one of perception; either way, we should know and use the chord tones.

There are two main types of modulations we should learn to recognize: *direct* and *pivot chord*. The direct modulation is easiest to spot: the first chord in the new key does not fit the previous key.

**Direct Modulation**

| C | F | C | B♭mi7 | E♭7 | A♭ma7 |
|---|---|---|---|---|---|
| C:I | IV | I | A♭:ii | V | I |

In pivot-chord modulation, the first chord in the new key is also a member of the old key. The two keys share the chord in common. In this example, G is the V of C, and it's also the IV of D.

**Pivot-Chord Modulation**

| C | F | C | G | A | D |
|---|---|---|---|---|---|
| C:I | IV | I | V | | |
| | | | D:IV | V | I |

When soloing through a key change, look and think ahead so you can change scales smoothly. We'll practice this in Part III.

# Part III:

## Chord-Tone Soloing Exercises

After Part II, we have enough information to (with practice) analyze note choices in relation to key centers and chords made by our favorite players and composers, and (with practice) make informed note choices of our own. Now we'll work on developing the reflexes necessary to apply them to the creation of our own music.

It's OK to move ahead while continuing to review the material in Part II. The exercises in this part are meant to reinforce the basics while further developing your musical senses. A reasonable practice schedule at this point might start with 10 minutes of chord, scale, and arpeggio study, then two 10-minute stints on one of the exercises described in the following chapters, with short breaks in between all. Finish the session with another 10- to 20-minute time frame that feels like a reward for your hard work: learning a tune or lick you know you'll like, a jam, etc. Keep those time frames strict, setting time aside to analyze new material you've learned so that you can apply its content to your own solos.

In this part we'll resume making melodic lines lead smoothly into chord tones, as we did in Part I. When this is done properly, our single-note playing sounds stronger, with a sense of inevitable movement toward resolutions. Even if no one else is playing the chords of the progression, they'll still be implied in our solos.

When any instrumentalist lacks this ability, it's pretty easy to recognize. It sounds like he's not really playing with the band and fitting the song. Suppose, as an audience member, you feel a change is upcoming in the music: an important chord move is happening, or perhaps one part of the song is ending and another one is beginning. The rhythm section builds toward it: the drummer plays a fill, and the bassist may "walk" up or down to the next chord, but the guitar player is blasting away on his favorite licks, which may be cool but have little to do with what the other guys are playing. He may even mis-time the transition, stepping on the vocalist's entrance, or finishing too abruptly, as if someone had run up and snatched the guitar out of his hands. These things can be fixed by practicing the ability to think of music as a linear sequence: the notes form a line that is going somewhere, in a very specific amount of time that you can learn to feel.

Why do I say "feel?" There is not enough time during a performance to plan lines like this by conscious thought. To get around this problem we have two methods: 1) we can compose and practice solos that fit the music, and 2) we can also train our reflexes to choose and play notes faster than we can consciously think during improvisation.

Both skills are important, and in the end a good soloist will have a very good idea what he/she will play, but by focusing on purely improvised soloing, we'll get better at playing composed solos, too. By training ourselves to be more time- and chord-aware, we'll know when to start and how to phrase the licks we've written or learned from others.

Thinking about the note or chord that is happening in the moment won't help except to help us keep our place in the music; we have to learn to look ahead. What chord is in the next measure? What are the tones in the chord? Which one should I aim for? How many beats until it gets here? Given the number of notes per beat that I am playing, which note should I be playing right now, in order to hit the target note on time? On a strictly conscious level it's usually impossible to know these things. But it's possible to develop instinctual awareness of them so we can make split-second, instinctual playing decisions. We'll practice this skill by **isolating** it, usually soloing over a metronome and whole-note chords only. Having bass, drums, and other instruments in the mix should come after we've established the ability to mark time between downbeats on our own.

Each of the chapters in this part contains an exercise to develop this kind of melodic facility and timing awareness, presented in roughly increasing order of difficulty. Though each chapter presents a new chord progression, you can apply any of the exercise routines to a progression from another chapter or to any song you need to play over, if it contains a chord progression of some kind that you can analyze.

Using more songs exposes you to more chords and situations. Jazz, pop, Latin, and R&B most consistently present opportunities to learn something new from a harmonic standpoint. A good source is a *fake book* of standard jazz and pop tunes. A *chart* (or *lead sheet*) contained in one of these books has melody and chords only, so one book can include a thousand tunes. Below is a typical sequence of tunes assigned for improvisation practice, going from easy to medium-hard, usually with about two weeks spent practicing each. These are mostly jazz standards, but working on them will make your soloing stronger in all styles, including rock and country. While you can use any songs you want, consider that a completely valid musical work can be hard to learn from because of its idiosyncratic nature—it may be operating on a plane other than the one you're focused on.

The Thrill Is Gone
Autumn Leaves
Blue Bossa
Tune Up
Solar
Four
All the Things You Are
The Girl from Ipanema
Joy Spring
Stella by Starlight

Make your own chord tracks with the metronome set at incrementally higher tempos for the exercises as you start getting better at them. If you have the capability to adjust the tempo without re-recording, remember to practice the chords at the new tempo. Try plucking the chords instead of strumming them, so that all the notes start at exactly the same time.

It's also totally acceptable to backtrack to a lower tempo any time you need to in order to perform the exercises. For maximum workout results, try to stay just below a tempo where the exercise is too hard. If you have days where that boundary seems to move down by itself instead of up, follow it; practice more slowly.

Sometimes you'll feel as though you're actually getting worse instead of better in the course of these exercises. This happens to everybody. New habits are forming on freshly laid neural pathways, which can make for some awkward and unpleasant sensations. At these times you are actually learning the most. It's only over the long term that you'll see drastic improvement, but rest assured, it'll happen.

# 3rds and 7ths

Back in Chapter 2 we played roots and 3rds as targets over a 12-bar blues, using triads in the chord track. Now we'll target 3rds and 7ths, again on a 12-bar blues, but the progression will be the more familiar traditional one using all dominant chords.

Memorize the chord changes of the blues progression with numerals so that you can play them in any key. There are many variations, but a basic version moves to the IV chord in measure 5, returning to I in measure 7, with V–IV–I–V starting in measure 9.

| | | | |
|---|---|---|---|
| I | I | I | I |
| IV | IV | I | I |
| V | IV | I | V |

A popular variation is the *quick change* to IV in measure 2.

| | | | |
|---|---|---|---|
| I | IV | I | I |
| IV | IV | I | I |
| V | IV | I | V |

Practice playing the chords for both the quick change and "slow change" examples in a few different keys, using dominant 7th chords only, letting whole notes ring for each measure. (Chapter 9 can help if you have trouble finding the IV and V chords in different keys.)

A common mistake with the blues progression is to start with two bars of the I chord, then go to the IV in measure 3. That can cause problems. If you don't use the quick change in measure 2, then you are locked into a slow change, which is just fine. Stay on that I chord while counting a full four measures.

## Half-Step Moves

When dominant chords move from I to IV or V, or back (from IV or V to I), the 3rd of one chord is a half step away from the ♭7th of the one that follows, and vice versa. The movement of a half step between tones of two chords is a smooth one, and is characteristic enough to imply the entire chord change by itself.

Play the next example three times. The first time, play the double stops: 3rds and ♭7ths together. (These are called *shell voicings*, or just *shells*.) The second time, play only the notes on the fourth string. The third time, play only the notes on the third string. The full chords and a blues bassline could start playing in your head just from hearing one note move.

| | 1 | 2 | 3 | 4 | 5 | 6 | 7 | 8 | 9 | 10 | 11 | 12 |
|---|---|---|---|---|---|---|---|---|---|---|---|---|
| Chord | G7 | C7 | G7 | | C7 | | G7 | | D7 | C7 | G7 | D7 |
| T (3rd string) | 4 | 3 | 4 | 4 | 3 | 3 | 4 | 4 | 5 | 3 | 4 | 5 |
| A (4th string) | 3 | 2 | 3 | 3 | 2 | 2 | 3 | 3 | 4 | 2 | 3 | 4 |

In dominant chords, the 3rd and ♭7th are always a tritone apart, and it's pretty easy to move the shapes to a higher or lower register.

The 3rds and 7ths of chords are called the *guide tones*. For this chapter's soloing exercise, we'll use these notes as targets and connect them with only one pattern of the minor pentatonic scale of the overall key: in this case, G minor pentatonic, pattern 4. (We're making it easy so we can concentrate on the targeting.)

Use a 12/8 (or *shuffle*) feel like the sample guitar on the track. A shuffle is like swing but even bouncier. Each of the four beats in each measure is divided evenly into three parts. You still tap your foot four times per bar.

The rhythm track for this exercise has bass and drums only—no chords. When you target the 3rd or 7th correctly, you'll provide enough of the chord for the listener to feel the progression moving. There are five choruses on this track. Listen to the examples on the CD track, then dial out the solo guitar and:

1.–3. Play lead-ins of gradually increasing length, using the G minor pentatonic scale, to either target on each chord.

4. After hitting the target with a one-eighth-note lead-in, add the root of each chord.

5. Intersperse the target notes with a few blues licks you may know, or improvise around the target notes with scale tones. Emphasize shuffling eighth notes played in time, with your foot tapping, so that it's easy to properly incorporate the targets.

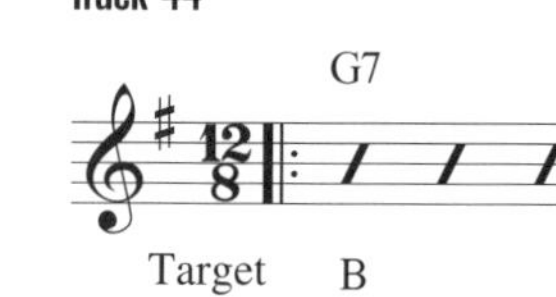

Track 44

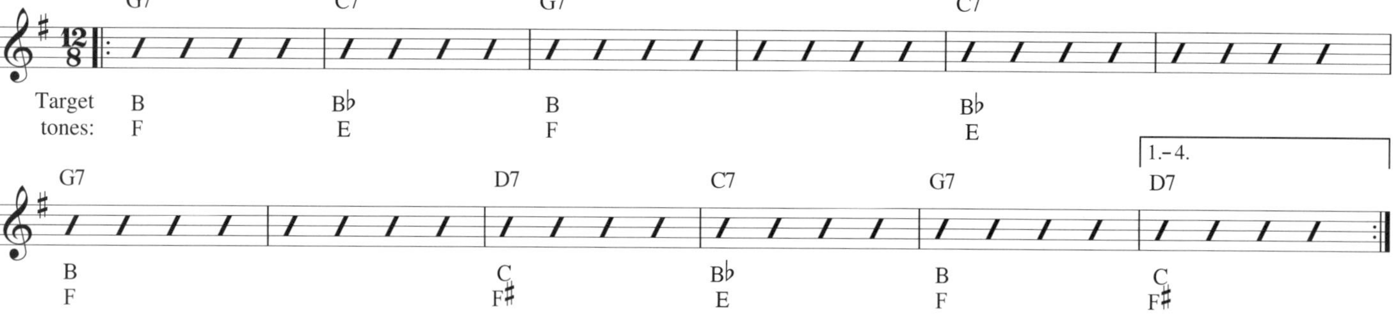

To review, by accenting a 3rd or 7th, we can imply the sound of the entire chord. The 3rds and 7ths in a traditional blues move mostly by half step, which is a harmonically strong movement. Half-step movement is also strong in diatonic progressions, which we'll see in upcoming chapters.

## Writing Assignment

Write out and practice a 12-bar chorus of simple eighth-note lead-ins so you can play them with consistency over the G blues progression. Use standard notation if you can. Only write it in tab if you can't read music at all. First, write in a target chord tone right after each bar line, and then put pickup notes immediately before it, one at a time. When you can play the part consistently, transpose it down a minor 3rd to E in open position, writing it out again. Make any adjustments needed to accommodate the open strings.

Composing solos will help you develop confidence, memory skills, and the knowledge that you have at least one chorus you can play that sounds good and applies the targeting concept. On the other hand, do not forgo improvisational practice, at which time you are forced to make instant decisions. Composition and improvisation are equally important. If you're playing a composed solo and something goes wrong, you want to be able to quickly recover and improvise from that point onward.

# 16 The Frosty Fretboard

If your car windshield is frosted over, you can clear one spot really well and see enough to get moving. That one small clear spot would be better than an entire window that is sort of foggy. Of course, you have to defrost it completely before you can be sure you won't get a ticket or wreck the car. The fretboard can be like that windshield. (Personally, I've never gotten a ticket for lousy playing, but I've caused plenty of wrecks!) When we have a new chord progression over which to create a melodic solo, eventually we want all of the fretboard to be clear to us, but we can get started by staying in a small area with one target note for each chord and learning that area really well. With time, we'll make our field of available notes larger.

Now we'll start using naked chord tracks so that we can focus on our timing. We'll go a step beyond the previous chapter's blues progression with a *minor blues* in C. This variation of minor blues has a ♭VI instead of V in measure 9, giving us four chords to deal with overall.

| | | | |
|---|---|---|---|
| i | iv | i | i |
| iv | iv | i | i |
| ♭VI | V | i | V |

If you analyze this chapter's chart as we studied in Chapters 10 and 11, you'll see this is a diatonic progression in C minor (with the exception of the major V). C natural minor is the scale of choice overall except the G7 in measures 10 and 12, where we may raise the B♭ to B♮ to fit the chord, changing the C natural minor scale to C harmonic minor.

Our clear spot on the frosty fretboard will be just a little more than one octave of C minor (including both B♭ and B♮). We'll use the notes we can reach in position on the top four strings only, from B♭ on the eighth fret of the fourth string to E♭ on the eleventh fret of the first string. We'll use pattern 4 of the scale, because it's closest to the chord voicings shown in the progression. Just review the top four strings of the scale pattern. Do not use strings 5 or 6.

7fr

C D E♭
G A♭ B♭ B
D E♭ F
B♭ B C

Within this small area we'll target the 3rd of each chord. (We could also target the 7ths.) The 3rd of Fmi (A♭) is a note that is definitely a change from Cmi (and is not in the pentatonic scale), so you'll know immediately if you play it at the wrong time. Torturing people like this is how I amuse myself.

Mark the 3rd of each chord on the chart so it's right there to guide you.

Now review the fretboard positions of the target notes within the scale. The objective is to connect these targets using the surrounding notes in the scale.

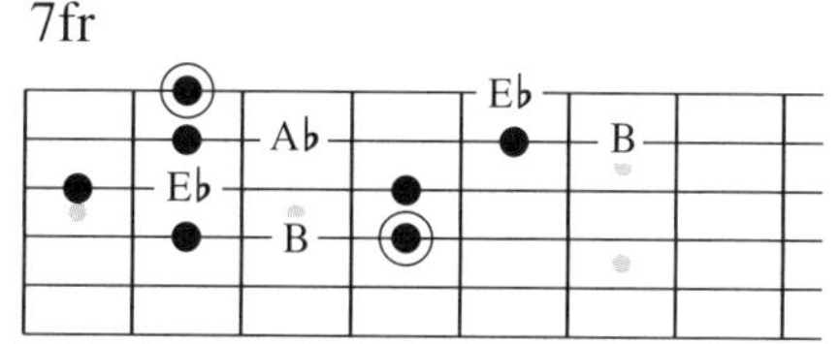

Use no bending, sliding, hammer-ons, pull-offs, or vibrato. Removing these, especially the vibrato, can be hard, but it's important to learn to control their use. Stay strictly within the natural minor scale with eighth-note attacks only, switching to harmonic minor for measures 10 and 12 only. Don't play any faster, and avoid any blues licks; we're trying to learn something new here. Remember to include the 2nd and ♭6th scale degrees in your line—don't just play the pentatonic scale. Again we'll have five choruses to play over.

**Using the CD Track:**

1. Practice the targets in whole notes through the progression until you can find them all on time.
2.–4. Play eighth-note lead-ins of gradually increasing length to the target notes using scale steps only.
5. After a single eighth-note lead-in (starting on the "and" of 4, right?), add another scale tone or two continuing in the same direction. This makes the targeting action more subtle, but it is still definitely there.

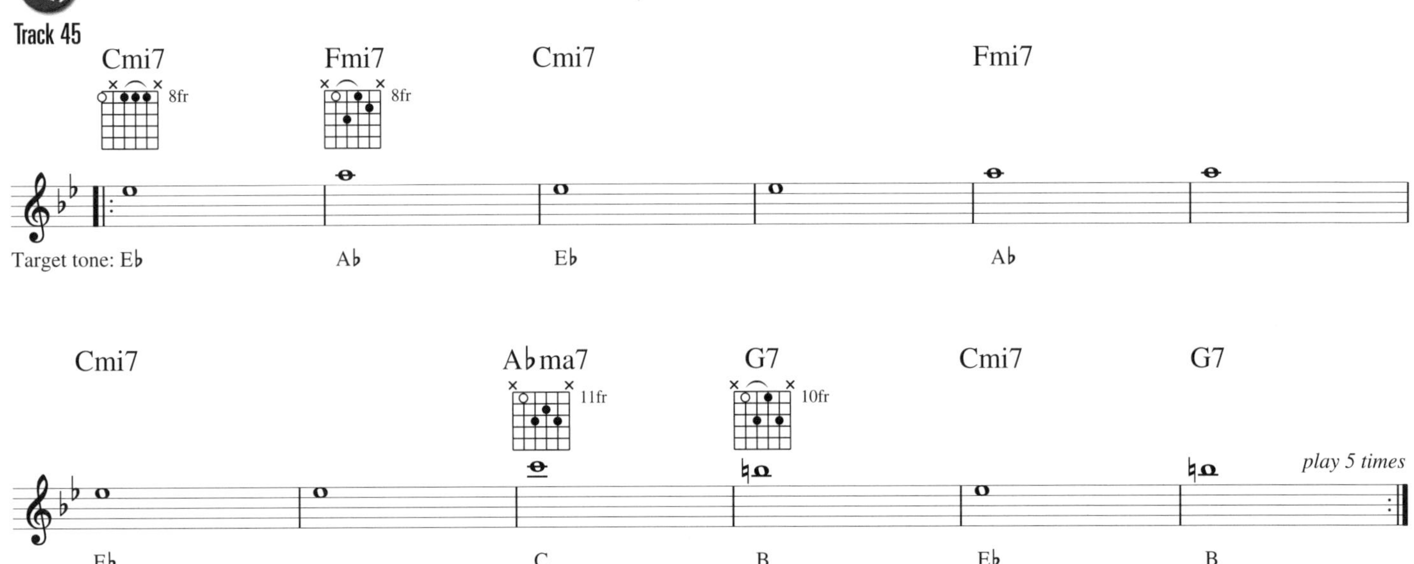


It's OK to stop to figure out where and when you have to start the lead-ins if necessary, or even write them out. But start playing in time with the track as soon as possible.

## Writing Assignment

Write out and practice a 12-bar chorus of eighth-note lead-ins with notes after the targets (as in step 5 above). Remember to use both ascending and descending lead-ins to the target notes.

When you can hit the targets somewhat reliably, you can then increase the size of your clear spot in the windshield. Add pattern 5 of the C minor scale above pattern 4. Also locate chord voicings for the progression in this position. (If you don't know the other patterns of the C minor scale and its diatonic chords, you'll need to review Part II to do this.) Find the 3rds in the new pattern and repeat the lead-in process.

It is not necessary to practice this chapter's progression in every single fretboard position, clearing the whole windshield before moving on. Better to expand your knowledge of typical chord progressions while practicing the targeting approach with the next chapter's topic, arpeggiation. I do suggest you stick with this exercise for at least two weeks, maybe four, with gradually longer lines and faster tempos. (Actually, when you see the next chapter, you'll wonder why you wanted out of this one.) For variety, apply the "lead-in-to-3rds exercise" to other chord progressions, getting to know a progression pretty well for a week or two, but not beating yourself up with it, before moving on to another one.

# 17 Arpeggiation

A solo consisting of nothing but strictly arpeggiated chords can sound great sometimes. An example is the fadeout solo choruses of "Hotel California" by the Eagles: the guitars repeatedly arpeggiate the song's main chord progression, hitting only chord tones. Other times, too many arpeggios can make a solo sound like an exercise. Most importantly, when we practice arpeggiating the chords in a progression, we're continuing to familiarize ourselves with locations for every chord tone so we can later use them as the basis for a variety of phrasing approaches.

When you have a new chord progression to play over, first find the root shapes for each chord in one position. Work out the arpeggio shapes from the root, ascending as high and descending as low as possible while staying in position. Try to minimize movement up or down the fretboard. Draw diagrams of the arpeggio shapes, labeling them with their pattern numbers. In this example, I have diagrammed the arpeggios for you in fifth position. At first, start each arpeggio from the root, reviewing the entire shape for each. With arpeggios, we know we're playing something that fits the chords because all of these notes are in the chords. When playing only chord tones, it's not even completely necessary to know the key center or scales (though we could use the G major scale on this progression, with A harmonic minor on the E7 chord). Chord tones always work.

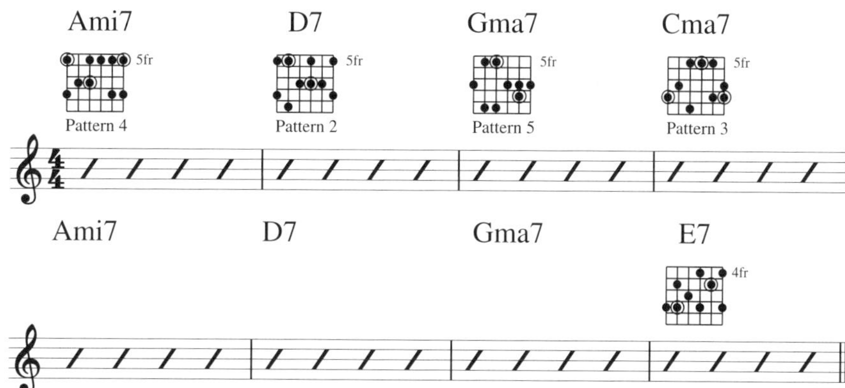


## Step Through, Then (Root) Dive In

For our first crack at arpeggiation, we're using a short progression that only contains five chords, though it does start with a ii–V–I, making it more sophisticated from a structural standpoint than the other progressions we've used so far.

Once you have reviewed the shapes, then "step through" exactly eight eighth notes of each arpeggio while slowly counting each note aloud: "*one and, two and, three and, four and...*" Do this all the way through once without the backing track. (The step-throughs on the CD are played in time at a very slow tempo so you can follow them.) This way, you'll have time to think about what you're doing. But don't stop there. Start playing the arpeggios in eighth notes along with the track before you feel completely ready. It's OK to make a few mistakes, as long as they're not the same mistakes over and over.

Track 46

Track 47

**Step-Through**

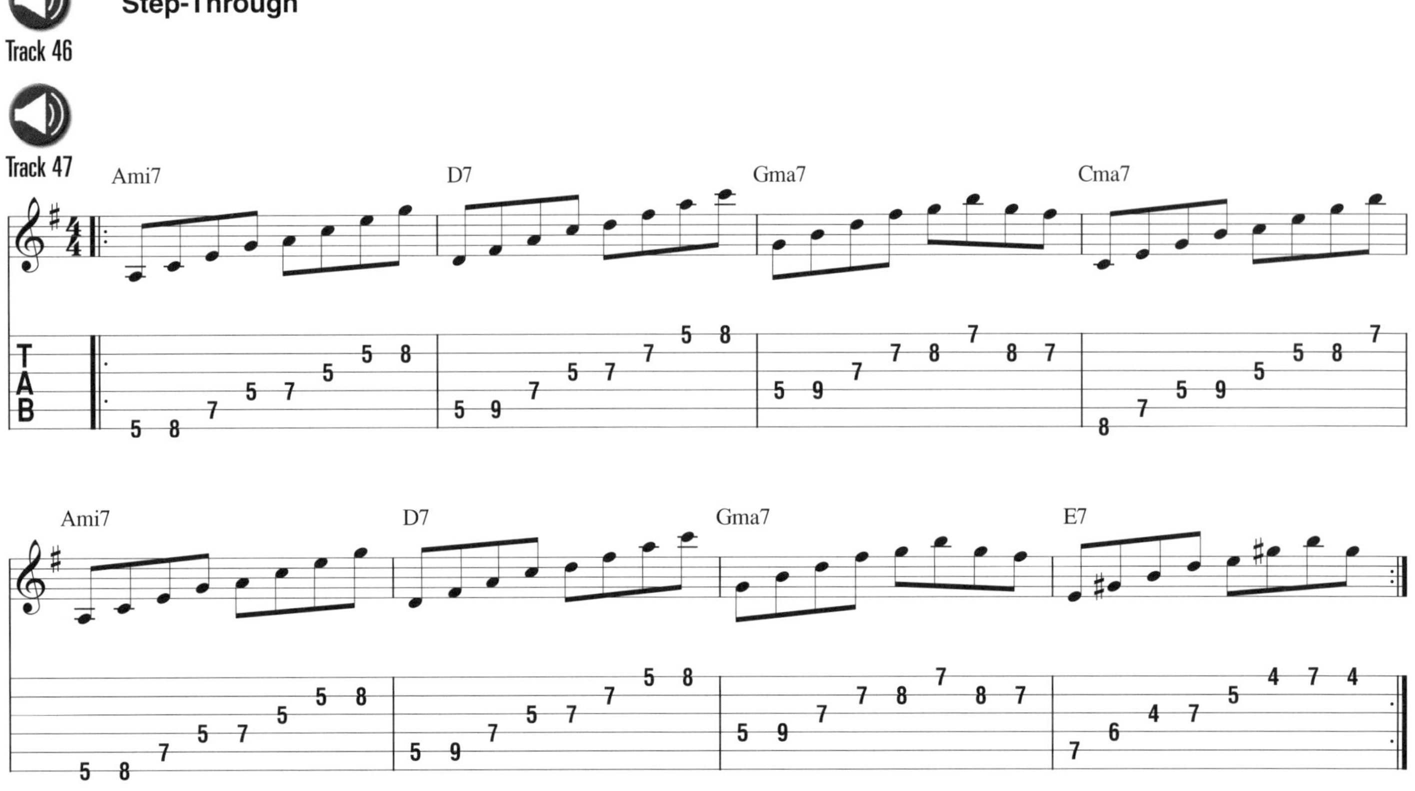


As soon as possible, you should be playing this without looking at the notes on the page. Here's a summary of the routine:

1. Review the arpeggio shapes in one position and practice them individually with the metronome.
2. Step through the progression without the metronome, counting eight eighth notes of each arpeggio.
3. Arpeggiate the chords in time with the track.
4. Increase the tempo of your own rhythm tracks very gradually.

Include this in your daily practice regimen only for as long as it takes to get familiar with the sequence of shapes.

## Arpeggio Connection

The previous was an example of *root diving*: wherever you are when the chord changes, you're diving from there down to the root of the next arpeggio, which we did first only to make it easier to learn the arpeggio shapes. Root diving is not a reflexive action we want to drill in from a musical standpoint, because it's too choppy and awkward. As soon as your root diving is seventy-five percent solid at a slow tempo (60–70 bpm), move on to smoothly connect one arpeggio to the next by the closest available note, while moving in the same direction (up or down), always staying within one fret of the fifth position.

We talked about this a bit in Chapter 9, but let's review what it means to say "by the closest available note while moving in the same direction." Let's say you happened to start an ascending Ami7 arpeggio in measure 1 from the root on the sixth string. The last eighth note of the measure is G on the eighth fret of the second string. On measure 2, you move to the closest note that is contained in D7 while still ascending: the A on the first string. You can ascend one more note without shifting position (C on the eighth fret), then you have to start descending. Make sure you understand the restrictions of the exercise, then practice it in step-through fashion, counting each eighth note aloud.

## Step-Through

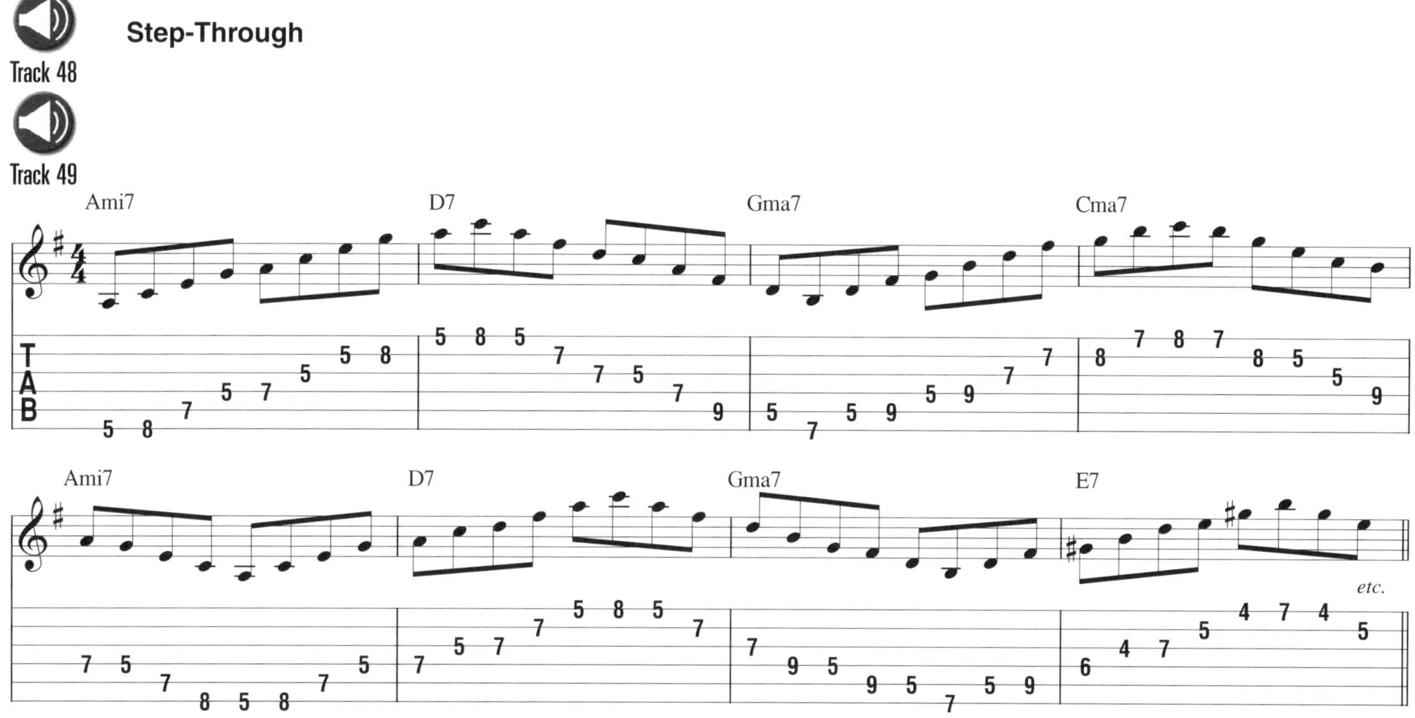


This is only a short example of the exercise as you will actually perform it. With each repetition of the progression, a different note of each arpeggio will be the closest available one when the chords change, making the exercise a little different each time through. Don't just repeat what's written here.

After stepping through, connect the arpeggios in time with the track. Don't look at the diagrams when you perform the exercise. It's easier if you memorize the arpeggio shapes first! If you've practiced your arpeggios starting from each string and the exercise still seems impossible, go back to counting and stepping through the arpeggios without the metronome, and write a chorus or two of the exercise out on paper, making sure you start on a different chord tone of Ami7 each time.

Now the daily practice routine might go like this:

1. Review the arpeggio shapes in one position and practice them individually, with the metronome.
2. Step through the progression, counting eight eighth notes for each measure, connecting the arpeggios by the closest available notes.
3. Connect arpeggios by the closest notes in time with the track.

Continue to practice arpeggio connection on other chord progressions. The songs on the list at the beginning of Part III are recommended, starting with "Autumn Leaves." Record your chord tracks in solid, unadorned whole notes along with the metronome at a slow tempo like those on the CD. This will make it clear exactly when the chords are changing and provide a backdrop for you to hear if you're hitting the correct notes and playing in time. The only difference should be that you make your recordings a full 10 minutes long (use the timer), so you can practice for 10 minutes nonstop. I recommend starting at a tempo of 60 bpm. Re-record the rhythm track (developing your chord-playing chops), increasing the tempo only a little at a time to keep yourself challenged, and writing down your metronome settings to track your progress. If you have multitrack equipment, record your solos and assess their accuracy. When you can play the exercise with few mistakes at a reasonable tempo (eighth notes at 100 bpm is enough for this exercise), you can then move to a different fretboard position and work out all the arpeggio shapes there, starting the connecting game again.

Arpeggio connection is hard work, especially at first; don't get the idea that there's something wrong with you. Just keep at it and you're going to improve. Once you get used to this routine, it's one of the fastest ways to get familiar with (and burning through) a new chord progression. Many professionals keep some form of arpeggiation in their practice on a permanent basis.

# 18 Targeting 1, 3, 5, or 7

The arpeggiation exercises showed us all the chord tones of a progression in one position. This time we'll play lead-ins, as before, only now we have all the chord tones—the root, 3rd, 5th, or 7th—to choose from as targets. We'll confine ourselves to one small fretboard area at a time, as before.

This chapter's practice progression contains two different key centers. For measures 1–8 and 13–16, use the same eighth-position C natural minor and harmonic minor scales we used on the minor blues. Measures 9–12 change keys to D♭ major with a ii–V–I–I chord sequence. D♭ major pattern 4 is positionally close to C minor pattern 4. Here are the two patterns on the top four strings only, side by side.

We'll also draw a picture of the two scales on top of each other, using O's for C minor and X's for D♭ major.

C minor = O
D♭ major = X

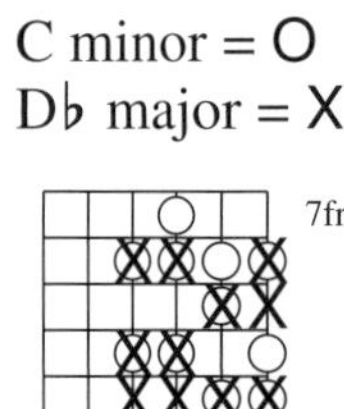


These scales contain five *common tones.* The two differences are D and G in the key of C minor compared to D♭ and G♭ in the key of D♭ major. First, play one scale, then the other, then repeat them both, noting how only these two pitches change while all the others stay the same.

When you're familiar with the scales, start the track and play non-stop steady eighth notes up and down the scales. Don't try to hit a lot of target tones yet; we'll do that next. For now, just familiarize yourself with the two scales and concentrate on switching between them at the correct time. Make sure you're really paying attention in measures 8–9 and measures 12–13: the transition areas from one key to the next. The key changes are somewhat abrupt, so strive for a smooth line moving through them. Not to belabor this, but **try not to stop playing** when the key changes. Mix out the example solos and play along with the CD track until you've got the switch happening.

Track 50

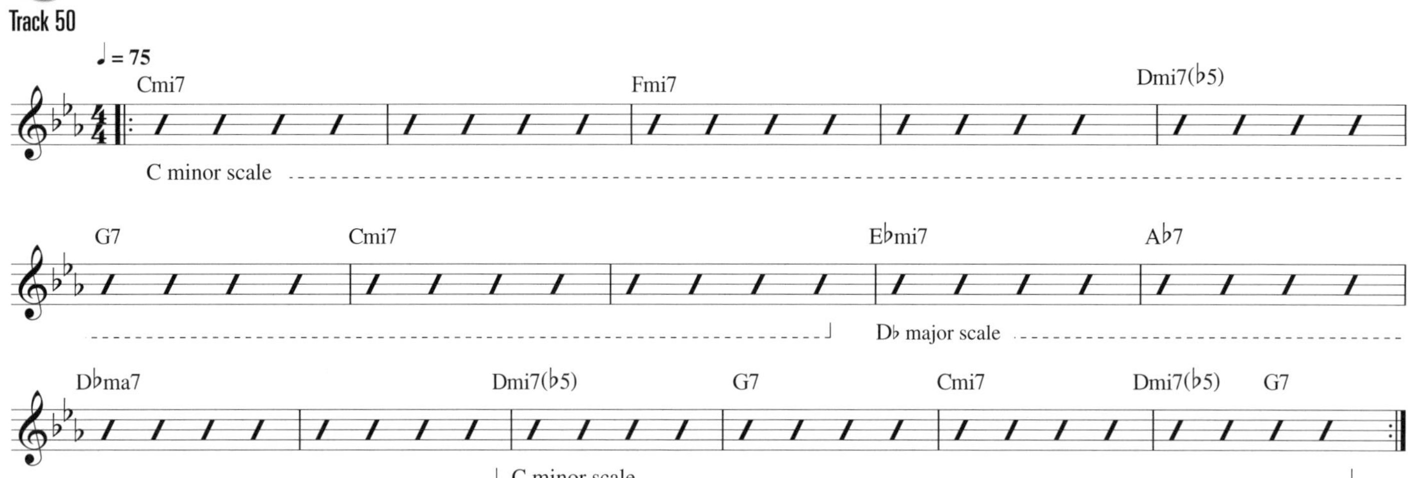

When you can switch smoothly between the two scales (as demonstrated on the first two choruses of the CD track), you're ready to include some chord-tone targets. Here are all the tones in each chord in this chapter's progression. We'll pick one tone as a target and write it beneath each chord.

**Chord tones in measures 1–8 and 13–16, C minor:**

| | | | | |
|---|---|---|---|---|
| Cmi7 | C | E♭ | G | B♭ |
| Fmi7 | F | A♭ | C | E♭ |
| Dmi7(♭5) | D | F | A♭ | C |
| G7 | G | B | D | F |

**Chord tones in measures 9–12, D♭ major:**

| | | | | |
|---|---|---|---|---|
| E♭mi7 | E♭ | G♭ | B♭ | D♭ |
| A♭7 | A♭ | C | E♭ | G♭ |
| D♭ma7 | D♭ | F | A♭ | C |

Track 50 (cont.)

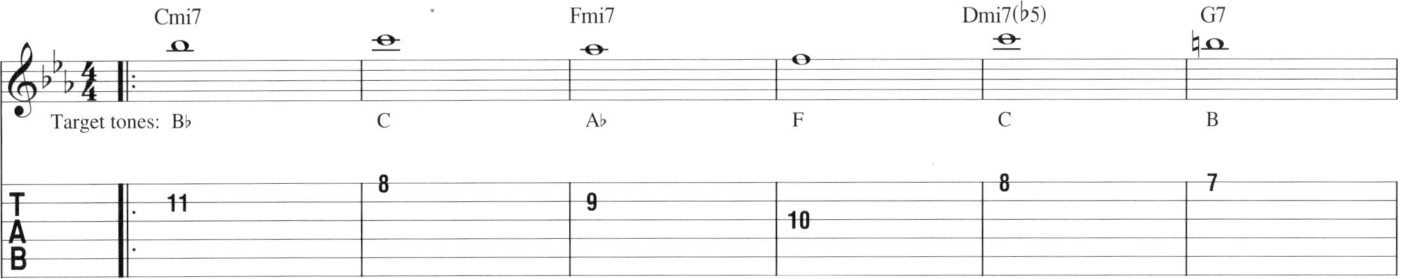


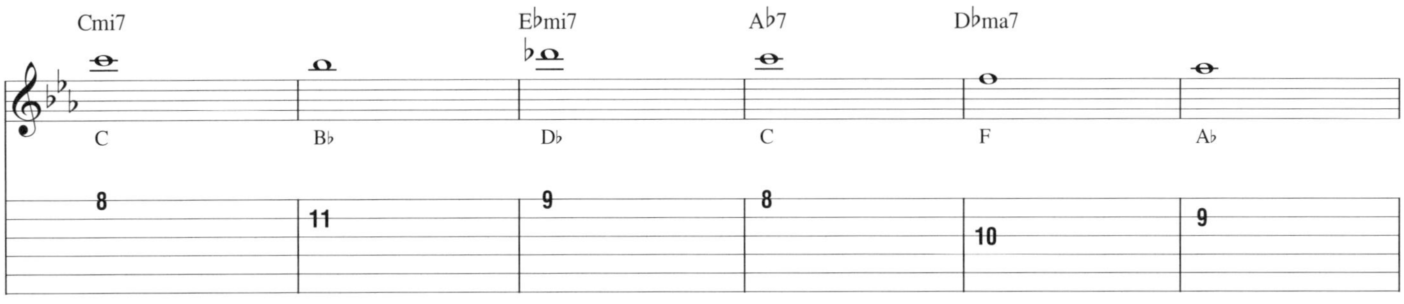


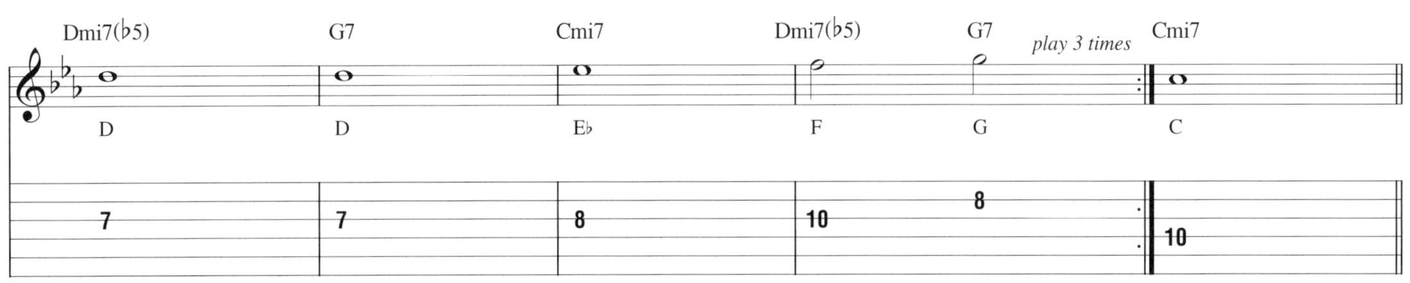

**The CD Track Demonstrates:**

1.–2. Nonstop scales, switching keys on time.
3. Two-eighth-note lead-ins to the target notes using steps from the correct scale, starting on the correct beat so that the target note falls on the downbeat of the chord.
4. A one-eighth-note lead-in, adding extra scale or chord tones after the target, so that the line now ends later than the downbeat of the measure.
5. Incorporation of the target-note approach into improvised phrasing over the progression, still using eighth notes as the basic rhythmic unit.

When you can hit these target notes at 90 bpm, change to different chord-tone targets, and perform the exercise again.

As well as consistent sessions, you need a quiet place to work with minimal distractions. It's best if you have a spot where you can leave your stand and charts up, ready to go as soon as you sit down, take out your guitar, and tune up. Try to practice at the same time of day, and for the same amount of time each day. If your practice schedule is usually one hour per day, and you happen to miss a day, avoid the temptation to put in two hours to make up for it. It'll make you think that you can just skip and then double-up like this all the time—and you can't.

# 19 Steady Eighth-Note Lines

Now we'll play rolling lines that move up and down the scale, yet still hit chord tones at the correct times. This exercise is similar to the short lead-ins we've played but has a more challenging non-stop pace.

In your continuous line, you may 1) change directions melodically up or down at any time, 2) skip over some notes in the scale, or 3) hit the same note twice in a row, in order to hit the targets on time. Strive to put these corrective devices (changing directions, skipping notes, or repeating notes) in the first few beats of the measure. Avoid them during the final approach to the target at the end of the measure, which you want to keep as smooth as possible for now. Do not add any non-diatonic (or *chromatic*) notes at this time. Stick with eighth notes only; there'll be time for lots of rhythmic variety later. Right now, we're still training ourselves to feel the spacing of measures, with eighth notes as the basic unit.

The chart contains two main tonal centers with a couple of short variations. First, measures 1–8 and 17–18 are D Mixolydian modal progressions, which you can see by putting the notes of the chords in alphabetical order (D–E–F♯–G–A–B–C). The D Mixolydian mode will fit over these two parts; though you may prefer not to emphasize the note C over the I (D6, D) and IV (Gma7) chords.

Second, there's a modulation to B minor in measures 9–16, with the opportunity to use the B harmonic minor scale in measures 8, 12, and 14.

In measures 19–20, we have a non-diatonic dominant chord (C7) that does not fit neatly into the D Mixolydian harmony, though it's a common chord move. The C7 can be analyzed as modal interchange (the ♭VII borrowed from D minor), giving us the D minor scale to play over it. C Lydian ♭7 (equal to G melodic minor: C–D–E–F♯–G–A–B♭) is another good choice on the C7 chord.

Warm up with the arpeggio connection exercise on the new progression, if necessary, in order to familiarize yourself with the chord tones in the fifth position (or any position you'd like to use). The sample target tones are written mostly at the fifth position.

First, step through the progression without the backing track while counting aloud and playing a line of continuous eighth notes. This is demonstrated on Track 51. Focus on hitting the targets with lead-ins that are as long as you can make them (from one to three eighth notes); the other notes can be any notes from the proper scale for the chord of the moment. Then start playing in eighth notes along with the next track.

There's not much time to think when you're playing, but mistakes are quickly forgotten in the pursuit of the next target.

Track 51

**Step-Through**

D Mixolydian

| | D6 | Gma7 | Cma7 | D | D6 | Ami7 | Cma7 |
|---|---|---|---|---|---|---|---|
| Target tones: | F♯ | B | E | D | A | C | B |
| TAB | 7 | 4 | 5 | 7 | 7 | 5 | 4 |

B harmonic minor
B Minor
D F#7 Bmi7 F#mi7 Bmi7 C#mi7(♭5) F#7 A7 F#7
D C# B C# D E A# C# E
A7 Bmi7 Cma7 Gma7 D C7 D6
D Mixolydian
D natural minor
G B B A B♭ C D
Track 52
D6 Gma7 Cma7 D
D6 Ami7 Cma7 D F#7
Bmi7 F#mi7 Bmi7 C#mi7(♭5) F#7
A7 F#7 A7 Bmi7
T
A
B

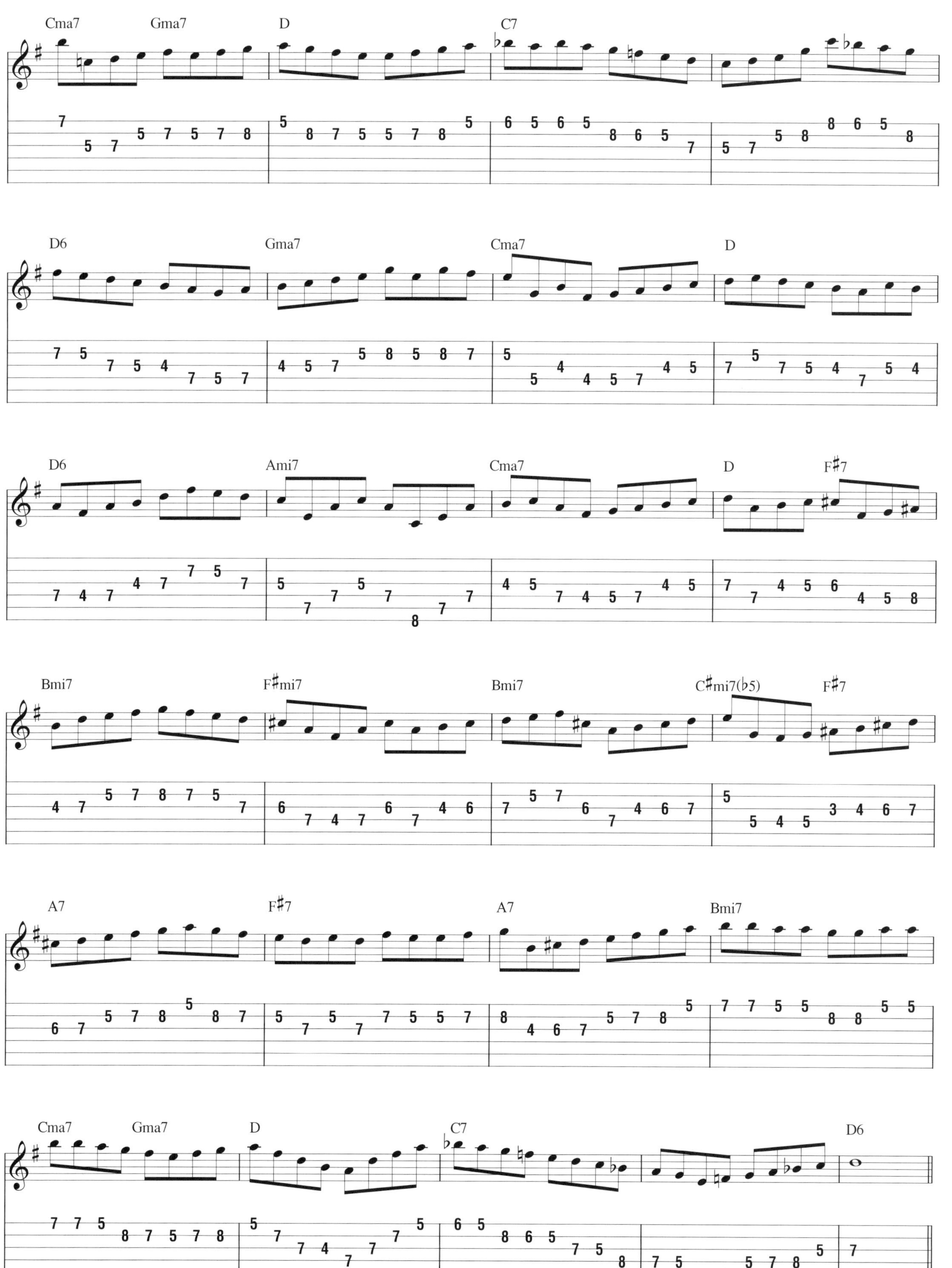
Cma7 Gma7 D C7
D6 Gma7 Cma7 D
D6 Ami7 Cma7 D F♯7
Bmi7 F♯mi7 Bmi7 C♯mi7(♭5) F♯7
A7 F♯7 A7 Bmi7
Cma7 Gma7 D C7 D6

In the course of playing these lines, resist the urge to cheat on the approach to the target notes. If you know you're about to miss one, don't speed up or slow down or stray from the scale in an attempt to prevent it. You'd build a bad habit by doing this. Fix your line if you can, but only within the eighth-note rhythm and within the scalar limits of the exercise. Better to let the mistake happen: hit a note that you didn't mean to, or hit the target early or late. Feel the pain, and do better the next time that part comes around.

You can apply this steady eighth-note exercise to other chord progressions, choosing a chord-tone target for each chord and writing it on the chart to reinforce the development of your on-the-spot analytical skills.

## Writing Assignment

Write out and practice a 20-measure line of eighth notes that applies the principles we've covered so you can play it with consistency over this chapter's progression. Composing the line is easier if you do some of it backwards, first writing in a target note and putting lead-in notes immediately before it, one at a time. This will eliminate some of the need to think ahead.

# 20 Scalar Connection to Any Chord Tone

After spending as much time as you need on the steady eighth-note exercise with single targets, use chord charts with all the possible target chord tones written in (or memorize them). Use the closest available tone in the next chord to keep your eighth-note line moving as smoothly as possible.

The smoothest line is one that continues in the same direction when it crosses the bar line of a chord change. This is desirable because it provides a thread of continuity over the changing chords. Then, while the chord is still sounding (and therefore not changing), the line can change directions to create interest in the middle of the measure.

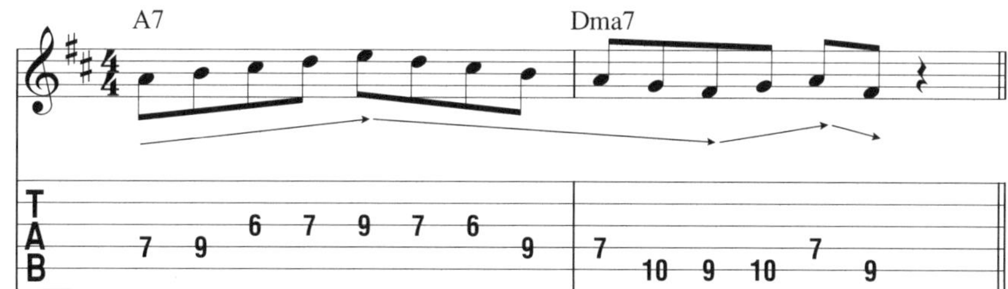


This chapter's progression contains three key centers: D, C, and B♭, always starting with the ii–V in each key. While it's best to learn to play all three keys with minimal position shifts, the "starter option" to use the same pattern number for each key does exist, moving down a whole step when the key changes. In other words, you could play pattern 4 at the ninth, seventh, and fifth frets for D, C, and B♭, respectively. Start this way only if you're still working on learning the five patterns.

In measure 15, we have a non-diatonic major seventh chord: B♭ma7. The preferred scale here is the B♭ Lydian mode, which will keep you correctly oriented over the chord. B♭ Lydian is equal to the F major scale, and both are equal to D natural minor, which is how we'd approach the B♭ma7 chord as an example of modal interchange (from D major to D minor). After a ii–V in D major, this is the ♭VI. Thinking in D minor is OK for this measure, as long as it doesn't come out in the form of a raunchy blues lick in D!

Listen closely to the example, then dial out the lead guitar on the CD and play your own lines.

**Step-Through**

Track 53

Track 54

| | D major scale: | | | | C major scale: | | | |
|---|---|---|---|---|---|---|---|---|
| | Emi7 | A7 | Dma7 | | Dmi7 | G7 | Cma7 | |
| Target tones: | D | G | C♯ | C♯ | C | F | B | B |
| | B | E | A | A | A | D | G | G |
| | G | C♯ | F♯ | F♯ | F | B | E | E |
| | E | A | D | D | D | G | C | C |

| B♭ major scale: | | | | D major scale: | | B♭ Lydian: | D major: | |
|---|---|---|---|---|---|---|---|---|
| Cmi7 | F7 | B♭ma7 | E♭ma7 | Emi7 | A7 | B♭ma7 | Emi7 | A7 |
| B♭ | E♭ | A | D | D | G | A | D | G |
| G | C | F | B♭ | B | E | F | B | E |
| E♭ | A | D | G | G | C♯ | D | G | C♯ |
| C | F | B♭ | E♭ | E | A | B♭ | E | A |

Scalar connection of chord tones may be the most difficult yet beneficial exercise in this part of the book. Practice it twice a day for 10 minutes each time (for a total of 20 minutes of actual soloing per session). After a few weeks you will feel some impressive improvements in your timing and musical awareness. When you go back and play with your usual phrasing, skipping strings and letting some notes ring, it'll have more power behind it.

## Writing Assignment

Write out and practice your own 16-measure line of eighth notes that applies the principles we've covered. Start by choosing a target chord tone for each measure, then fill in the other notes.

## Sounds Great. Can You Leave It Out?

After working with the exercises in these last few chapters for some time, you'll find yourself playing non-stop notes more than you'd like, and targeting a tone of every chord you see. This is fine for a while, because you've just acquired a completely new set of tools, and you're learning how to use them. To a man with a hammer, everything looks like a nail. But once you're sure you always know which notes you can play, it's time to go back and take some out! Because so much of playing is reflexive, melodic breathing space must be programmed in like anything else.

At this point, I think you understand how these exercises work: a chord progression is analyzed, scales and target notes are identified, and then a clear objective is repeatedly pursued over it in a controlled way until it becomes second nature. I now want you to engineer your own exercises where you practice playing sustained notes or rests on specific beats, even resting for entire measures at a time. An example might be: "I will play swing eighth notes, targeting 3rds and 7ths. For beats 2 and 3 of every second measure, I'm not going to play but rather count and rest." This is demonstrated in the next CD track (also over this chapter's progression), but again, you should think about it, make up your own rhythmic variation, state it clearly, and practice it.

Track 55

## More Writing

In addition to improvising within the parameters you've described for a 10-minute stretch, write out and practice a 16-measure solo chorus that follows the same rules.

# 21 Ascending Arpeggios and Descending Scales

This exercise is chord-tone targeting taken to the extreme, using nearly every beat as a resolution. When practicing these lines, review the nearest chord shape of the same quality as the arpeggio, with the same extension(s) if possible. The lines are written mostly in patterns 4 and 2 for easy learning, but as usual, they should be applied in all positions.

Each permutation of the exercise is a musical phrase you can use while soloing. It uses a basic jazz principle, but it will not make you a jazz player per se; the same approach can be used anywhere a harmonically sophisticated sound is appropriate, be it rock (classic and some pop), country (western swing, rockabilly), blues (jump, swing), etc.

Use a swing feel for these lines. The amount of swing will vary with the tempo: as the tempo is increased, the amount of swing gradually decreases, until at very fast tempos (300 bpm and over) it disappears completely, resulting in even eighth notes.

We'll ascend on the arpeggio and descend via the related scale, with the chord tones in the scale placed on the strong beats. The first example climbs a five-note A9 arpeggio, then descends on the A Mixolydian mode, with every strong beat (1, 2, 3, and 4) getting a chord tone. Because only every other note in a scale is a chord tone, this means each weak beat (the "and" of each beat) gets a non-chord tone.

You may start with either the arpeggio or the scale (reversing the order of the two measures), making the example a repeatable loop.

Track 56

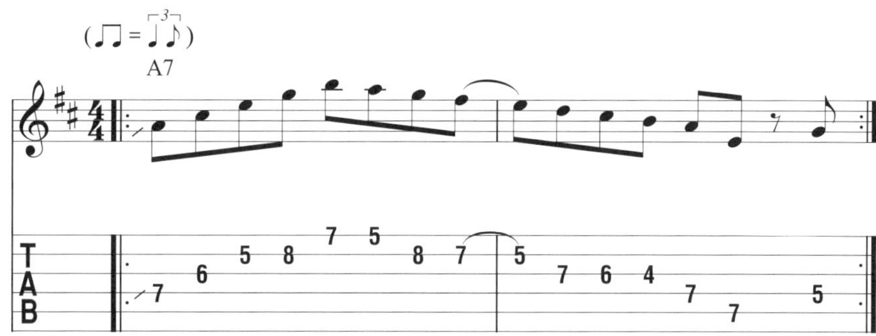


Now let's extend the arpeggio to the 11th. In this case the arpeggio ends after six notes. Then in the second measure, something important happens. If the scalar part hits any chord tone (except the root) on a weak beat—as it does on the "and" of beat one of the second measure—it means all the chord tones that follow on the way down will also be on weak beats, unless we do something to fix it.

Track 57

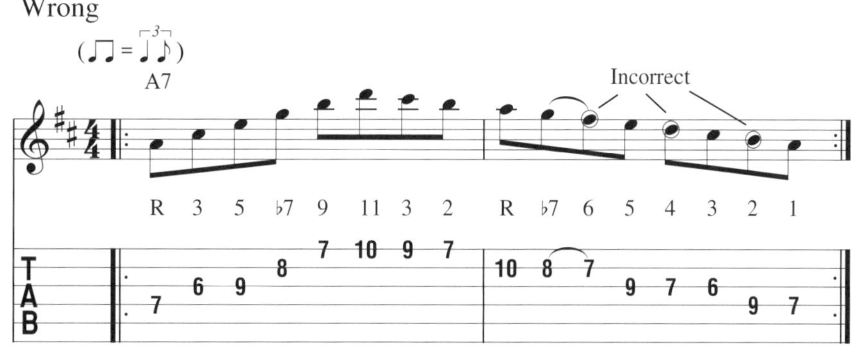

That example was incorrect for the purposes of the exercise (and it ended one note too early). The usual solution is to add a chromatic note, especially between the root and the ♭7th, resulting in the *bebop dominant scale*: 8–7–♭7–6–5–4–3–2–1.

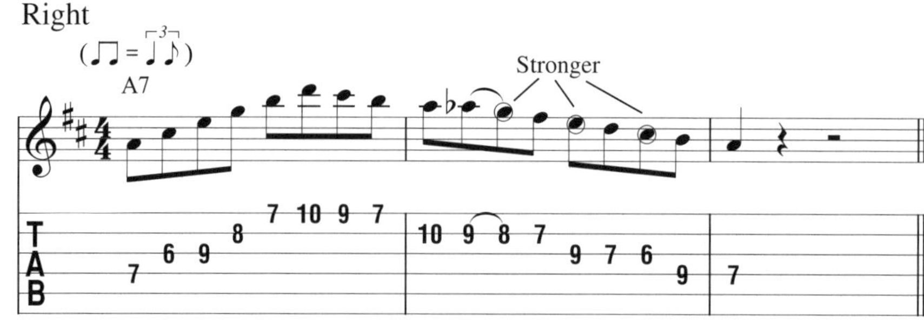


Now the line resolves properly on each beat, and it can be easily looped for practice.

Just to make it clear, here's the rule about placing that chromatic note in there: only use it when necessary to move the chord tones onto strong beats! If you start throwing in chromatic notes willy-nilly, you'll sound like the calliope at the circus. These notes are secondary to the main purpose of making a flowing line and should be used sparingly in the beginning, not as a crutch.

Of course, the arpeggio may start on a note other than the root and on a weak or strong beat, so you won't know in advance whether the chromatic note is needed until you get near or into the scalar area in the line. Practice very slowly while counting aloud so you can learn to hear it on the fly. Here's the A9 arpeggio again, but starting from C♯. Because the root is on a strong beat (beat 3), we need the A♭ after it so the rest of the chord tones fall on strong beats, too.

The extended arpeggio may be sequenced for practice, then followed up with the line to finish. Here's a dominant 13th arpeggio in groups of four.

Track 60

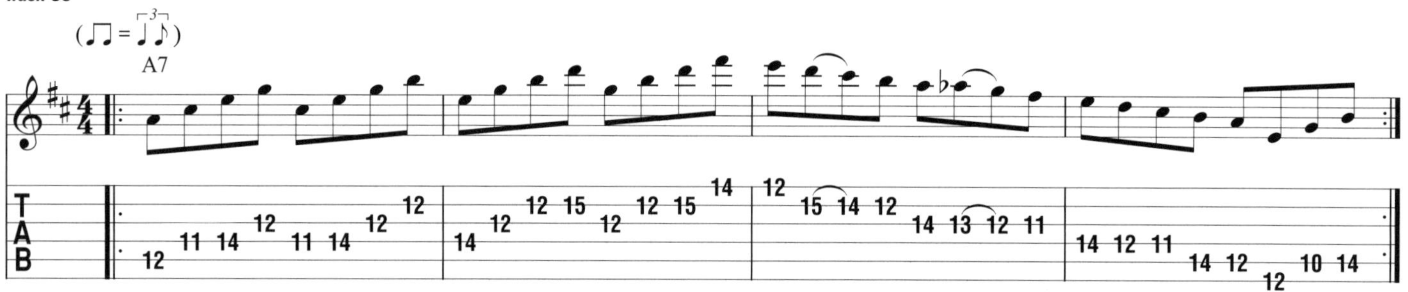


Over minor chords (usually ii in the key), we can use the same scale, the bebop dominant of the related V if the minor chord is a ii. The chromatic note falls between 4 and ♭3 on the way down the Dorian mode. It's a major 3rd over a minor chord—usually something to avoid like the plague—but when played exactly on the weak beat in between the 4th and the ♭3rd in a descending scalar passage, it's very musical.

Track 61

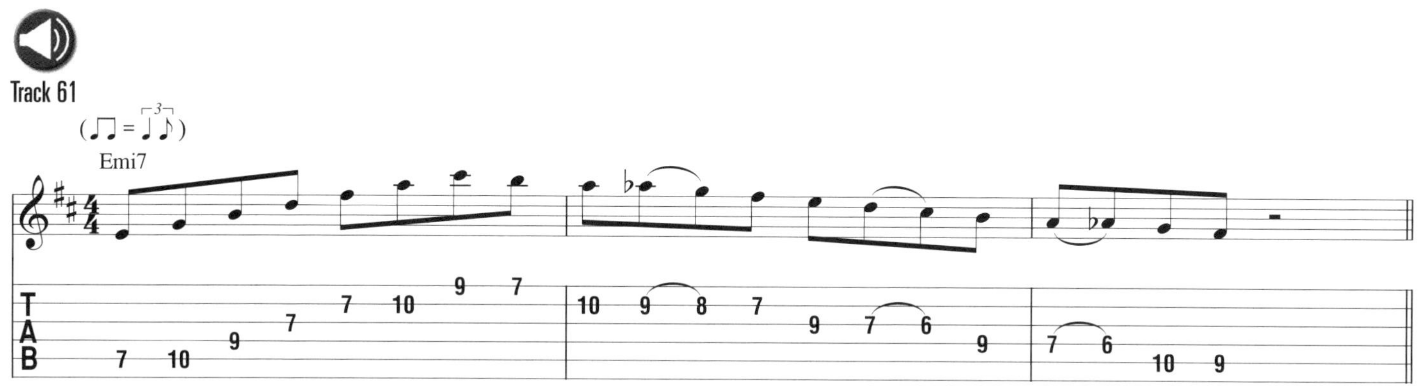


Wondering if you can put E♭ in the descending scale? Try it, but remove the A♭ that follows.

Over major chords, we can descend via the *bebop major* scale, which has the chromatic note between 6 and 5.

Track 62

Track 63

Track 64

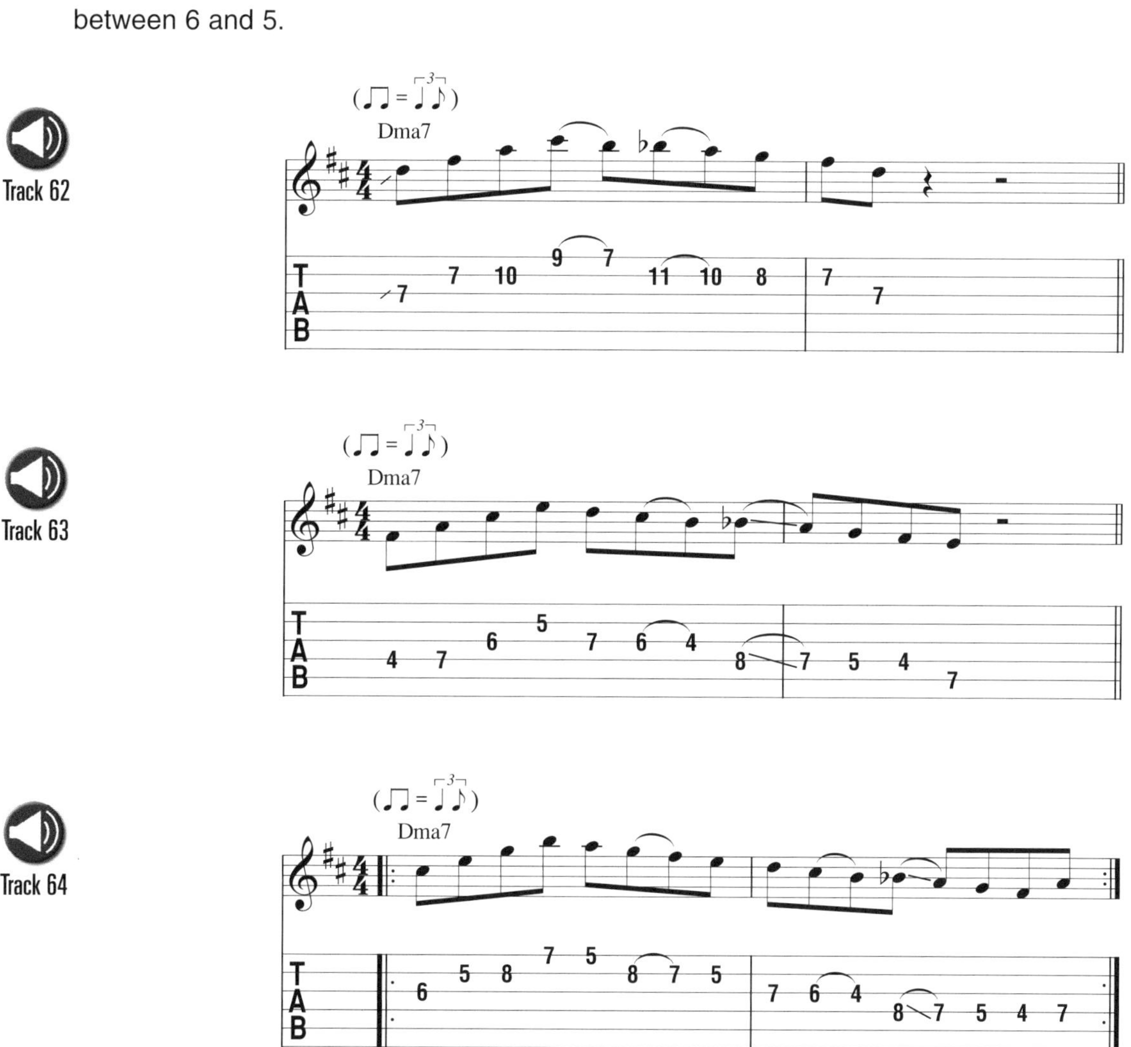


Another solution that is sometimes better than a chromatic note is a melodic skip (seen here on beat 4) that lines up the 7th on the strong beat: we skip to A, then descend from C♯.

Track 65

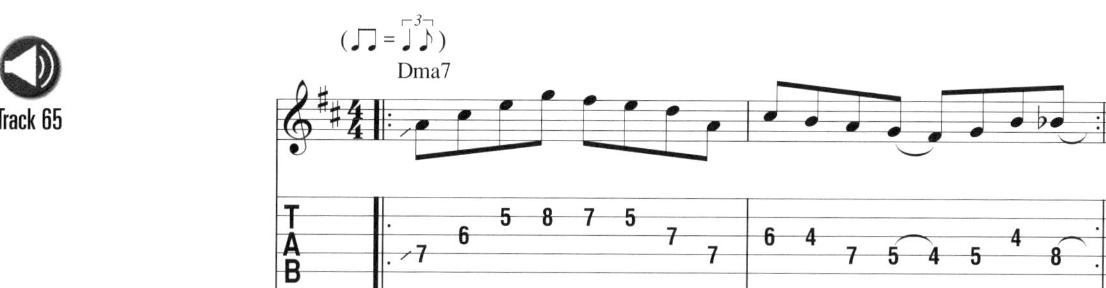

## Altered Arpeggios

Scale and arpeggio passages over altered chords should generally contain those same alterations. In particular, the V7 chord in a minor-key progression requires that extended arpeggios be altered. Here's a B7 arpeggio, the V in the key of E minor with altered extensions. This arpeggio draws its tones and extensions from the E harmonic minor scale, which is also the descending scale that completes the exercise. With this chord, tension and dissonance are what we are after, so non-chord tones on strong beats are OK. The only note to avoid hitting on a strong beat during B7 is the root of the i chord (Emi) that follows, because it'll prematurely resolve the line.

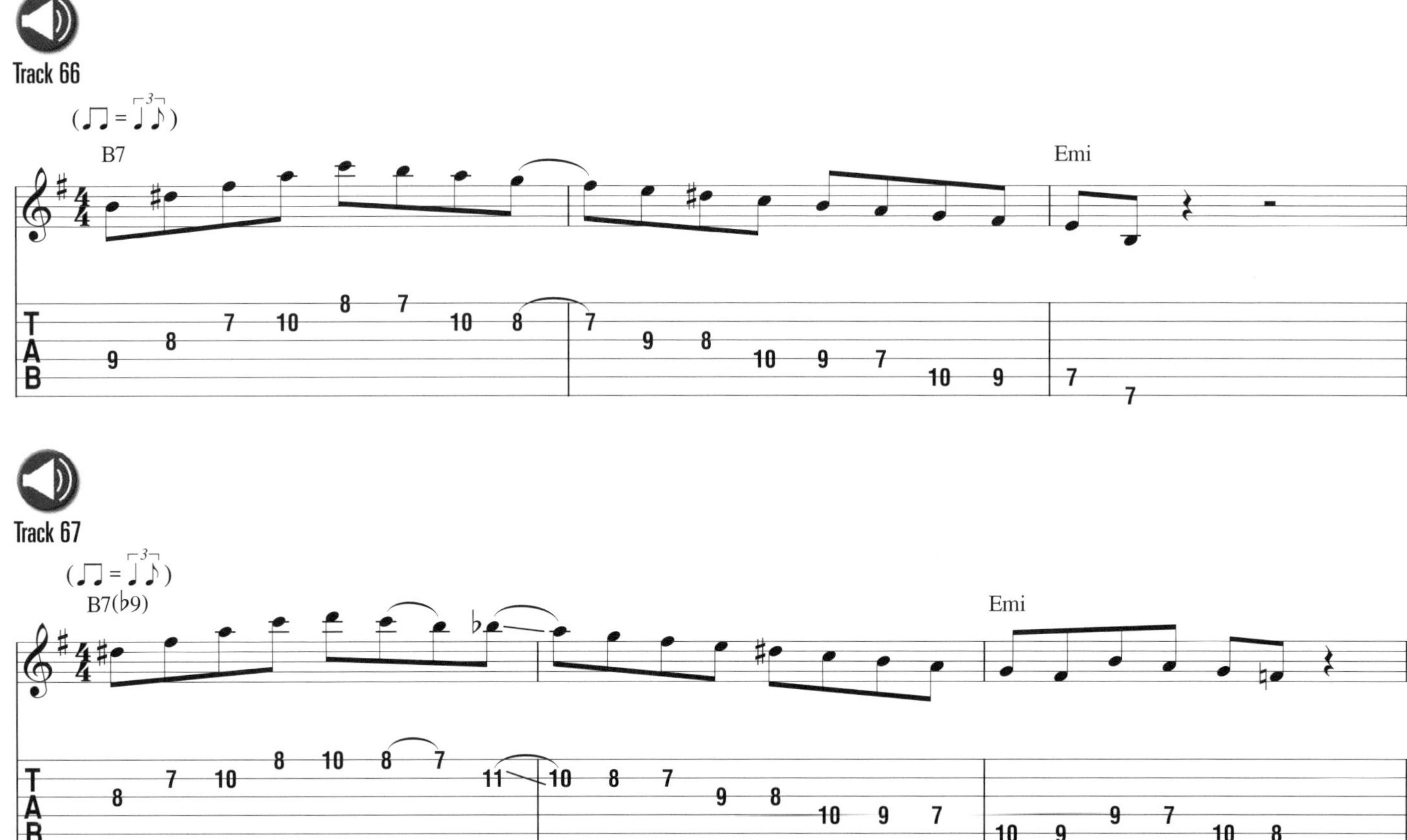


Notice the F♮ at the end of the line over the Emi7 chord. This is a jazz practice: the "wrong" note should usually be on a weak beat, and of short duration.

Track 68

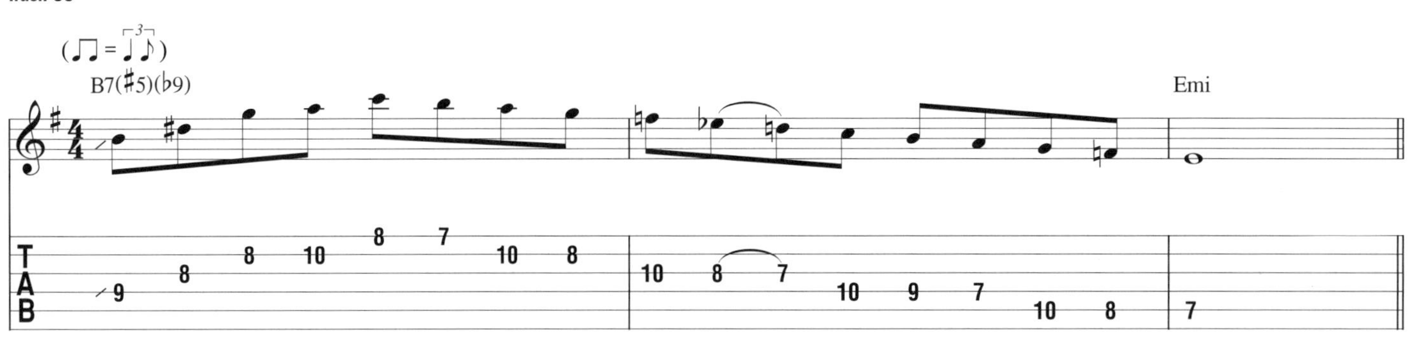


All of the exercises in this chapter only dealt with one chord at a time when possible, so we could get familiar with the basic concept of ascending arpeggios and descending lines before applying it to progressions. Nonetheless, this chord-scale approach is always affected by the key center we might be in.

# 22 Choosing Your Targets

Besides just using the closest available tone in the next chord to keep a line moving smoothly, we can also decide which note to play over a chord or within a phrase based on the stylistic or melodic effect it produces. A basic consideration when choosing a melody note is whether it tends to create a feeling of tension (wanting to go somewhere) versus resolution (being there). In some cases, we also influence the nature of the chords themselves by choosing notes or extensions that complete the modality (the sensations of major, minor, and the other modal flavors) or that change it from the one implied by the chords.

Earlier (in Chapter 9), we saw that a note can be analyzed simultaneously in terms of the overall key center and in terms of the current chord. Both are important, with the consideration of the overall key center usually taking precedence. For example, if you're soloing over multiple choruses of a 12-bar blues, playing the 5th of the overall key center in measure 12 will give the audience the correct impression that the song is not over yet, even in the case when there is a I chord instead of a V chord in measure 12.

Beyond basic guidelines like this, the choice of which note to play—be it chord tone, extension, or non-chord tone—over a given chord at a particular spot in a progression depends on the song, the style, and expectations created by earlier notes in the melody. This is where your artistic sense comes in. We cannot make a rule to say, "Always play the root here; always play the 9th there." It doesn't work like that.

## Melodic Guide Tones

A good way to learn (or should we say, discover) your preferences as to which notes to use at a particular time is to analyze what was played by others in relation to their chord progressions. Do this as closely as you can in conjunction with learning the melodies and recorded solos note-for-note. As a type of practice that helps us apply what we've learned, we can extract the essential melodic notes used and make them our target notes during improvisation.

These notes can be called guide tones for our purposes (up to now the term *guide tones* has been used to mean 3rds and 7ths only). These guide tones are the notes that would still suggest the basic melody even if the ones around them were taken away. We can also imitate the places where the original melody has rests or sustained notes, letting our lead voice breathe while the groove of the rhythm section gets the listener's focus. The empty space in a melody is just as important as the notes.

Following is a chord progression consisting of six four-measure phrases: three for the verse, and three for the chorus, for a total of 24 measures. Over these chord phrases are melodic phrases that are repeated with slight variations while the chords change beneath them. The melodic phrases in the verse are just two measures long, with some four-measure melodic phrases in the chorus to provide contrast and a buildup of energy.

Adding to the challenge, some chords are *anticipated* (played earlier than usual) by an eighth note, which you'll usually want to accommodate in your soloing. Targeting tones on *syncopated* (off-beat) chords requires you to pay close attention to your counting.

Review the recommended scales that are written above the chords; guide-tone targets from the melody are written below.

**The CD Track Demonstrates:**

1. The melody, as written.
2. Embellishment of the melody using riffs based on the target tones and repeated phrases.
3. A solo chorus using some of the same target notes an octave higher, but with more energy (more and higher notes).
4. Return to the original melody with a few embellishing phrases for interest.

Track 69

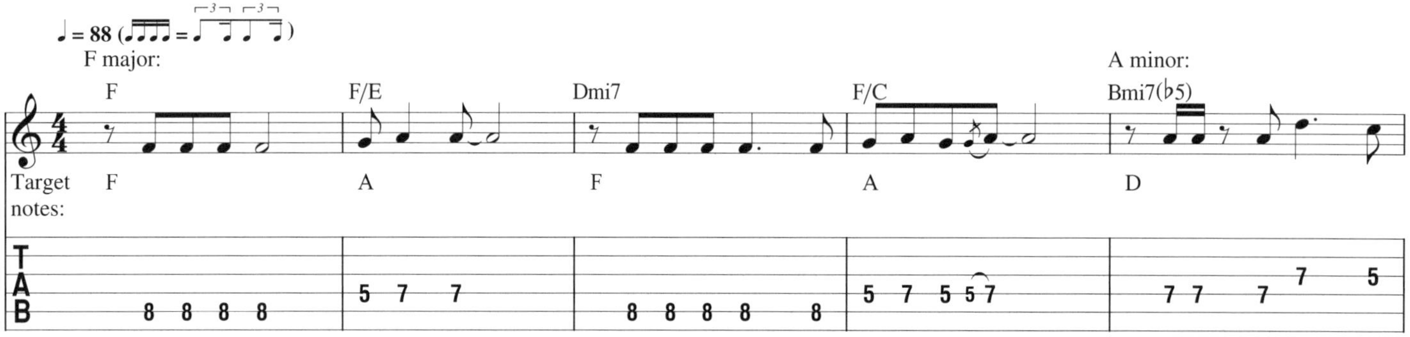


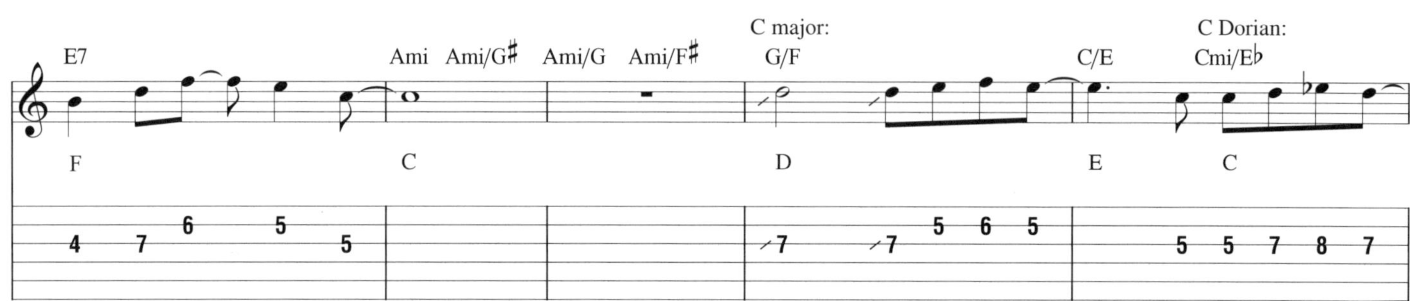


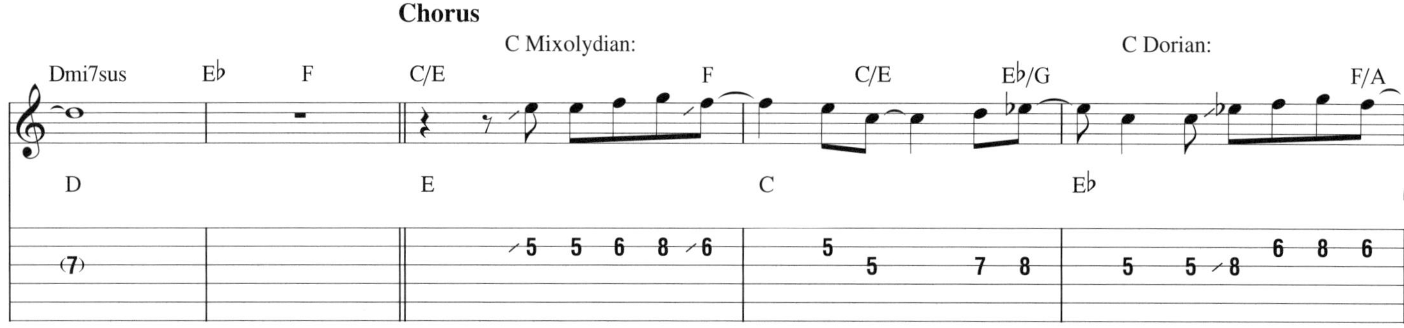


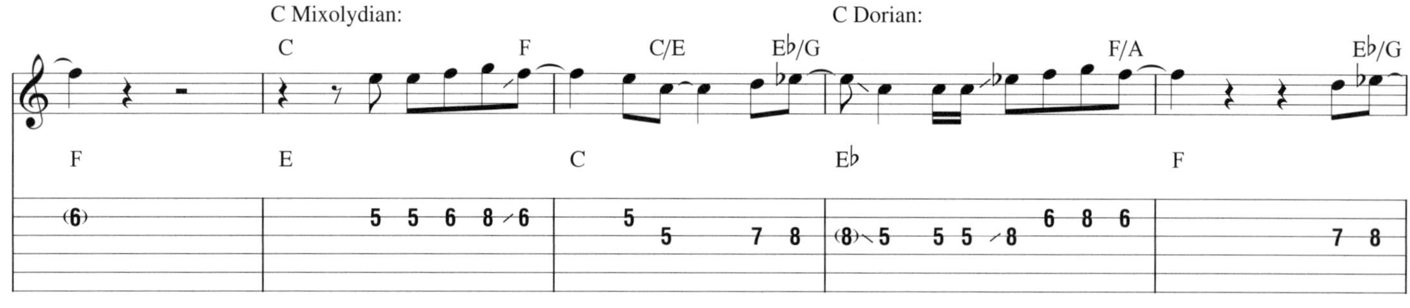

To Coda
C Mixolydian:
F/A
C
B♭/C
F
E♭
F
E
F
F/E
Dmi7
F/C
Bmi7(♭5)
A
F
A
D
E7
Ami
Ami/G♯
Ami/G
Ami/F♯
G/F
F
C
D
C/E
Cmi/E♭
Dmi7sus
E♭
F
C/E
F
E
C
D
E♭
F
E
C/E
E♭/G
F/A
C
F
C
E♭
F
E
C
E♭/G
F/A
E♭/G
F/A
C
E♭
F
E♭
1/2
1/2

C
B♭/C
3rd Time Solo
F
F
E
B♭
F/E
Dmi7
F/C
Bmi7(♭5)
E7
Ami
Ami/G♯
Ami/G
Ami/F♯
G/F
C/E
Cmi/E♭
Dmi7sus
E♭
F
C/E
F
C
E♭/G

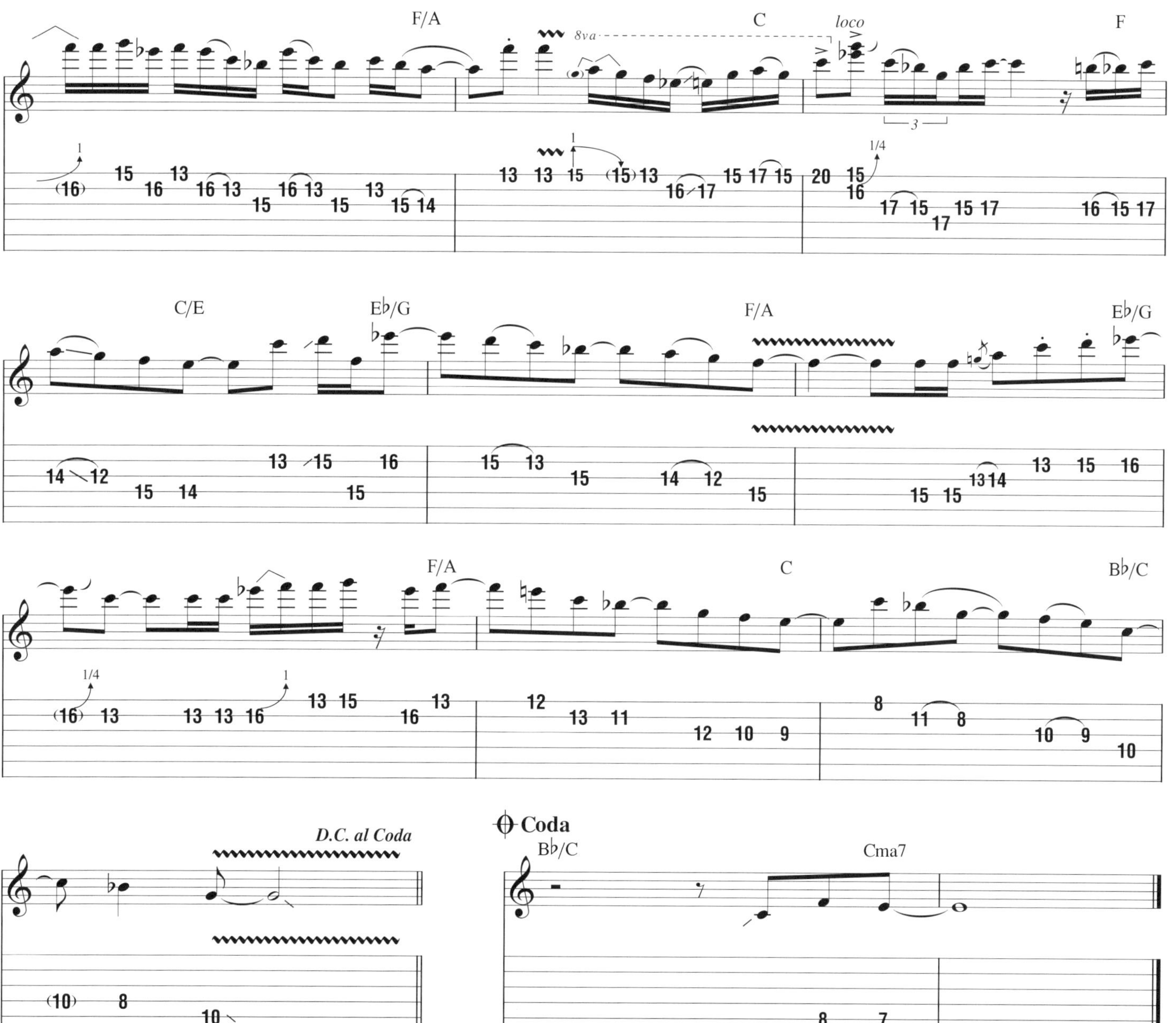


Notice how the energy level of the solo chorus decreases in the last six measures or so, giving a cue to the listeners and the rest of the band that the solo section is ending. The length of this tapering-off would vary depending on the song—usually somewhere between half and two-thirds of the way through the section is good. It's better to starting bringing things down a little early to be sure you don't overlap the singer or another soloist.

You may also create a guide-tone solo that uses different notes from those in the original tune. Try to pick target notes that create a simple melody that you could easily hum over the progression. You can choose any note or extension of the chord, keeping in mind that a good melody generally fits the phrase lengths described by the chord progression (most often two, four, or eight measures).

To facilitate note choice, you can 1) strum each chord briefly and then play the guide tone you're considering, 2) play the chord while singing or humming the note you're considering, or 3) find a voicing that features the melody note you're considering as its top note. Whichever note you decide on, write it on the chart. Find all the target tones in one position on the fretboard so you don't have to jump up and down the neck. Apply the various soloing exercises, incorporating your guide tones. Record your solo, if possible, as well as listening as you play, and change any tones you don't like to ones that sound more musical.

# Conclusion

I suggest keeping some type of tone-targeting exercises as set forth in Part III of this book in your practice regimen on a long-term basis. Add more challenges as you go:

- continue to target chords that change on beats beside beat 1 or 3 of the measure
- play lines consisting of triplets (three notes per beat), sixteenth notes (four notes per beat), or a mixture of the two
- use scale sequences and melodic ideas that fit or overlap chord phrases
- target chord tones over progressions that use odd time signatures
- apply phrasing ideas you've learned from other players
- think of some of your own ideas and practice until you can toss them in at will

An idea for a song may pop up while you're exploring a new exercise. It's also important to continue learning and analyzing solos and melodies by other players, so you can absorb the pacing, phrasing, and structure, as well as the fun part: stealing the licks.

It's been a pleasure for me to work on this book, and I sincerely hope these practice routines help you as much as they have me and my students. Good luck.

# About the Author

Barrett Tagliarino has been an MI instructor since 1987 and was Rock Department Head at Hohner MusikSchule in Vienna, Austria, in 1994. This is his fourth book for the Hal Leonard Corporation. Barrett has recorded TV and radio commercials and a Starlicks instructional video, *Classic Rock Guitar Soloing*. Barrett has also written articles in magazines like *Guitar Player* and *Guitar One*, and released an independent CD, *Moe's Art*. Find out more at his website, *monsterguitars.com*.

# Acknowledgments

I'd like to thank Tommy Gunn for playing the drums and Jason Moussa for testing this book. Thanks also to everyone at the Hal Leonard Corporation.